Calling All Angels!

Also by Joyce Keller:

Complete Book of Numerology
An Astrological Guide to Your Guardian Angels
Your Angel Astrology Love Diet
Your Angel Astrology Guide to Health and Healing

Calling All Angels!

57 Ways to Invite
an Angel Into Your Life

By JOYCE KELLER

ADAMS MEDIA CORPORATION
Avon, Massachusetts

Published by
Adams Media Corporation
57 Littlefield Street, Avon, MA 02322 U.S.A.
www.adamsmedia.com
ISBN 13: 978-1-58062-429-9
ISBN 10: 1-58062-429-4

Printed in Canada.

J I H G F

Library of Congress Cataloging-in-Publication Data
is available from the publisher.

This publication is designed to provide accurate and authoritative information with regard to the subject matter covered. It is sold with the understanding that the publisher is not engaged in rendering legal, accounting, or other professional advice. If legal advice or other expert assistance is required, the services of a competent professional person should be sought.

— From a Declaration of Principles jointly adopted by a Committee of the American Bar Association and a Committee of Publishers and Associations

Cover photo by The Vatican Museums and Galleries, Rome/Superstock.

This book is available at quanity discounts for bulk purchases.
For information, call 1-800-289-0963

To my very special angel, Jack

CONTENTS

ACKNOWLEDGMENTS

pecial thanks to my agent and friend, June Rifkin Clark; my editor, Pam Liflander; my radio station manager, Joey Alcarese; Grace and John Zemba; Dr. Scott Joseph Keller; Elaine, Jim, Alex and Nick Beardsley; Dr. Diane Zemba, Lorraine, and Johnny; and "Fred, the Man of International Mystery." A tremendous thank you to my husband Jack, who always inspires me, and who almost never loses patience with me when I have computer problems. Thanks also to my angels, who woke me up one night and asked me to stop writing a book about love, money and sex, so that they could help me write this one instead.

INTRODUCTION

The "Angel of the Airwaves . . ."
Welcomed me into the light
From far away, I felt the glow
  of her encouragement
And in my heart I felt the warmth
  of all the love she sent.

—An anonymous radio listener

n my lifetime, it has been my privilege to have served God in a variety of ways. One of my favorites has been as a radio and television talk-show host. For the past ten years, I've had the pleasure of speaking on the air with thousands of people. I've listened to their problems and intuitively tried to give them hope, encouragement, and direction. There has never been a moment of time while I've been on the air that I felt that I did not have angelic help and guidance.

There were many times that I listened to callers express the depths of human despair. As I listened, I wondered what I should say. What would be the best response? What did this person need to hear? What would be the most help to them? What would the rest of the audience think and feel about my response? What would my radio station's management think? What about the sponsors?

Usually while I was wondering about all of this, answers started coming out of my mouth. As I listened, thought, and spoke all at the same time, I realized that what I was saying was, indeed, what the listener needed to hear.

What's even more strange is that I always knew that the answers weren't coming just from me.

I knew that much of what I was offering the audience was coming from God's messengers—the angels.

Calling All Angels!

For he will give his angels charge of you
  to guard you in all your ways.
On their hands they will bear you up,
  lest you dash your foot against a stone.
You will tread on the lion and the adder,
  the young lion and the serpent you will trample under foot.

—Psalm 91, Holy Bible,
Revised Standard Version

1

Seven Ways to Receive Help from Angels

ngels give us hope. Just about everyone believes in them. Surprisingly enough, they are nonsectarian, and they don't offend anyone. Believe it or not, angels will help anyone who ask! However, their answers can be subtle that we may miss their message. Ho do we successfully communicate with angels so that their message or work for us will not be lost or misunderstood? I've provided some answers, I believe, in this book.

Most of us have heard that angels are all around us, and that they are just waiting to help us. Sometimes, though, we wonder why they are so hard to reach. Why aren't our prayers always answered? Why don't we have more evidence of their presence and assistance?

The response to the above question is that we don't really know what their angelic rules are, and how we need to follow those rules for meaningful communication.

I try to be very God-centered in the spiritual counseling work that I do. I believe I have been privileged enough to have had angelic communication and guidance for many years. I feel that angels have clearly shown me what most quickly and easily gets their attention. I understand what gets them to respond to our requests. I know their guidelines for successful communication and interaction.

Angels are loving, supportive beings of light and energy. They grow by serving humankind—but as with most things, there are rules and secrets to use when requesting angelic assistance. These easy rules and secrets are right here, and if you follow them carefully, you will see the magical results.

One word of warning, however. There may be times when angels are unable to help when we ask—times when we have to learn one of life's lessons. These are the only times they will not, and cannot, come to our aid. I believe, though, that prayer will always help to make these difficult lessons more bearable.

Seven Methods to Open Yourself to Angelic Assistance

I have used the following seven methods to facilitate my angelic communications, and I believe that combining these ways leads to greater openness to angels and the divine. They are prayer, the use of mantras, meditation, keeping your mind in the proper attitude, cultivating an angelic atmosphere, the use of angel-attracting materials, and through the use of crystals or gems.

The Power of Prayer

Do you sometimes feel
That prayers are not heard?
Know that God and His angels
Receive every word.

Whether shouted or whispered
From a heart that's broken
Our Lord's ear
Hears every word that's spoken.

Angels always at the ready
At God's right hand
Waiting . . . then forward charging
Ever at His command.

—Joyce Keller

Prayer is when we ask God and His angels for something; meditation is when we listen silently for a response.

When attempting to make angel contact, begin with prayer. Ask in your prayer to contact the highest, most helpful and interactive angels. Then ask for their help, and they will hear and respond to your call. Visualize yourself bathed in white light during all prayer and communication sessions.

Angels cannot answer prayers without an okay from God. Prayers are heard in heavenly realms by scores of angels, all ready to go and to serve. Still, *nothing* can be done without the go-ahead signal from the Big Boss. Remember the old adage, "You should be careful about what you pray for because you just might get it"? This may be another reason that prayers are not always answered.

Prayer, or asking aloud, is the key, and faith is very important. Know in your heart that angelic communication is your God-given right.

Do you think that your prayers are heard or not? According to recent research, over 60 percent of the American public believes that they are.

If you have not already read it, I heartily recommend Betty Eadie's book *Embraced by the Light*. Pay particular attention to her description of the way prayers are heard in the heavens. She says that prayers go up to the heavens in streams of white light or beams. Thousands of angels observe these upward streams and answer them at the command of the Creator. The strongest beams are those sent up by mothers praying for their children.

Powerful Star Prayer Technique

I've been fortunate enough to have known many spiritual giants. One of these special people is a Roman Catholic priest named Father Maurice Boucher. Father Boucher is the spiritual head of the awe-inspiring St. Anne's Shrine at Isle La Motte, near Burlington, Vermont.

He recently explained to me the importance of understanding the four points of prayer, which are represented by the word *star*. The explanation is simple—yet profound and extraordinarily powerful. Each time you pray, begin by thinking of the following:

> *S* for supplication. Ask humbly, with simple, strong faith, for what you desire.
>
> *T* for thankfulness. Have gratitude in your heart and mind for all that you have received and are about to receive.
>
> *A* for adoration. Feel and express love and devotion for the Creator.
>
> *R* for repentance. Ask for forgiveness for anything that has troubled your conscience.

Repetitive Prayer

I know the power of repetitive prayer. When I became a student of Swami Vishnudevananda of Montreal, Canada, and New York City, he gave me a personal mantra, or prayer. The prayer was "Om Na Mo,

Vashu De Vaya." It basically means "praise be to God." It was to be repeated many times a day, counting the repetitions on a prayer necklace called a Mala.

The effect, which required about fifteen minutes to achieve, was phenomenal. I usually fell into a deep prayerful state in which I instinctively knew that my prayers were being heard and considered by God and His angels.

The same effect can be achieved by the chanting of the word *Om*. Try going through the musical scale until you find a note that feels right to you. Repeat, drawing the word out—particularly the *m* sound.

My mother always taught me to say the Lord's Prayer or Psalm 23. Many people know from experience that repeating prayers by rote, such as the Rosary, is also reliably powerful. It is my feeling that using the Rosary is like using a cosmic telephone to dial the feminine principle of God, or the Universal Mother. While saying the Rosary, I can intuitively feel the presence and the response of the Divine Goddess. I sometimes feel myself surrounded by an electrifying blue-green light and feel Her powerful presence. I almost always feel Her close by when I repeat this prayer, and I can clairaudiently "hear" Her asking me, "Yes, my child. What may I do for you?" Anyone saying prayers that he or she feels deeply—or, in some cases, not so deeply—will in some way find those prayers to be uplifting or helpful. They need not be "standard" prayers from an established religion; they can be from your own creative thoughts, and the more heartfelt, the better.

Recognize and use the power of prayer. It will assist you in accomplishing all that you desire and in attaining all that you need. Have faith in your heart. Know that all prayers are heard. They're just not always answered as quickly as we would like, or necessarily the way we had in mind! Prayer should be at the root of all angelic communication.

Angel Mantras

Angels love simplicity and are drawn to words that rhyme.

The mantras in this book are simple, powerful rhymes that came to me during meditation. They are words of power that will help connect you with the highest power in the universe! Angels will listen and respond to the sound of your voice, especially if you speak in rhymes. Each of the angel mantras came from angelic realms and carries with it the correct vibration and energy to be effective. These angel mantras are also powerful because the type of angel being called is included: All beings are more responsive when they are addressed by their title.

The mantra that you need can be memorized or carried with you on a three-by-five card. Repeat it throughout the day until you receive a response.

I cannot overemphasize the importance of three other words of power: *please* and *thank you*. It is imperative that all angelic requests are preceded with the word *please*. Of even greater importance is finishing all sessions with *thank you*—even if it seems to you that nothing angelic has occurred. Believe in your heart and soul that these three words are magic! Angels will respond to your courtesy.

These angelic mantras work best when spoken aloud, whenever possible. They also work well when taught to children. The mantras are listed in chapter 3.

Meditation

Do you have the patience to wait until your mud settles and the water is clear? Can you remain unmoving until the right action arises by itself?

—Lao-tzu, Chinese philosopher and
founder of Taoism, 604–531 B.C.

Meditation, which is also known in metaphysical teachings as "going into the Silence" or the "gateway to heaven," is key to communicating with God and His angels.

Meditation is the stilling of the conscious mind; it can make possible an inflowing or downpouring of cosmic energy. Meditation also strengthens the connection between us and our Higher Powers—the invisible connecting "silver thread" that breaks at the moment of death, called the "sutratma" in Vedantic teachings and the "life thread" in Western philosophy.

Meditation increases creativity and intelligence by clearing away the heavy, dense vibrations of the Earth. It can ground someone who is flighty and not adequately centered. Meditation links us to the highest power in the universe.

One way of understanding the process of meditation is to think of a lake that is murky from a great deal of activity. When the action on the lake stops and things grow quiet, the lake becomes more and more crystal clear. Finally, it is perfectly clear; it is easy to see through it to the bottom. When this moment occurs in meditation, it brings increased awareness and clarity of thought. In addition, the reward of many years of disciplined, controlled meditation may well be the enlightenment of the soul, also known as "universal consciousness," "cosmic consciousness," or "knowing God."

Daily meditation—usually for fifteen to twenty minutes twice a day—causes positive changes in our consciousness. At first we might not notice anything at all, or we might simply notice that we are less stressed and possibly less irritated by our environment. Perhaps we are more intuitive, or maybe there's just more of a "knowingness," or understanding.

Don't look for immediate results, though. The products of meditation can be so subtle that you might think your efforts are futile. Don't give up!

Eventually, after steady, disciplined meditation sessions, you will begin to reap the rewards of being in touch with your inner self. It may require weeks, a year, or more. The length of time and results of your meditation can vary widely.

After months of steady meditation, however, you may suddenly experience a breakthrough. Perhaps it will be a flash of light, or a sunburst of color when you least expect it. Perhaps you will hear the roll of distant thunder or the sound of faraway bells.

One of the earliest and most pleasant experiences I've had during meditation is what I would call a "crown of light." During a very deep state of meditation, I occasionally experience what feels like a light hat placed on my head and a visual show of beautiful white flashes and streaks. I experience this on deep, internal levels, not physical. The feeling that comes with it is of jubilation and well-being.

Meditation is most effective when done at the same time and place each day. Try meditating in keeping with the Earth's cycle, which means at dawn and dusk, to harmonize with the Earth and its energy. Each session should last fifteen to twenty minutes.

Some people find it useful to have music to help them focus, and there are many uplifting meditation tapes available. However, I personally don't like to listen to music, since I find it anchors my energy too much in the physical realm and so keeps me from soaring. I would rather have complete silence and feel free to leave my body.

Cosmic Meditation for Angelic Communication

Sit comfortably, with a straight spine, to allow a free flow of energy. If you can sit in a yogic lotus position, that would be ideal. Try a straight-backed chair, or sit on the floor with your back to the wall for greater comfort. However you sit, though, try not to fall asleep.

Always have a large glass of water nearby, which after meditation will be poured out. I recommend that water be discarded after meditation or after sitting on a night table next to your bed while you've been sleeping. The reason is that water has the ability to draw into itself negative energy, and should then, of course, not be consumed. It is important to drink water after meditation, or upon awakening from sleep, but it should be fresh and clean.

If you wish to burn incense, consider patchouli, sandalwood, or Indian cedar rather than fruit scents; the former three are usually considered the most cleansing and uplifting.

If you burn a candle, choose a white one. You may even wish to try "flame gazing": Stare into the flame of a candle until you are able to see or feel angelic contact.

Begin by closing your eyes gently. Roll your head around your neck slowly . . . three times to the right and three time to the left.

Always begin with a prayer of protection. I suggest the following:

> *I surround myself with the highest;*
> *I surround myself with the white light of our Creator;*
> *Nothing but the best can come from me;*
> *Nothing but the best can come to me.*
> *I give thanks.*

Ask your angels to come to you.

Take three long, slow, deep breaths, in and out through your nose. Listen to the sound of your breath. If your mind starts wandering, repeat these three breaths until you feel greater control over it.

Begin the actual meditation process by visualizing a bright beam of white light. Like a searchlight, it comes down from the heavens and shines directly into the top of your head. As it touches, see your head flooded with white light. Then watch the light travel down the front of your body, filling every part of your being and flowing out from your feet. See this bright beam of white light come back up into your feet and travel up your legs to the base of your spine.

As it touches the base of your spine, it illuminates the first chakra. (The seven chakras are invisible psychic-energy centers, or "wheels," that run along the spine; one of the goals of meditation is to energize, or charge, these wheels, to allow clearer angelic communication.) Now see the beam of light continue up your spine, touching and energizing your second chakra, which is directly above the pubic bone. Next the light slowly travels to the chakra at the level of the solar plexus. Watch this third chakra begin to softly glow with white light.

Let the beam of light continue to rise to the fourth chakra, which is actually centered in the heart; it is the place from which love emanates. See it brightly illuminated. The light will continue to travel up your spine to the fifth chakra, in the throat.

Watch the beam of light continue upward and touch the Third Eye, or sixth chakra, which is located between the eyebrows and about an inch to an inch and a half up on the forehead. This is a particularly important chakra because it relates strongly to angelic communication. Let your consciousness linger here for a few moments. Now try to visualize what your guardian angel looks like. Try to actually "see" the face of an angel.

Hear the following Sanskrit words, and let them go deeply into your heart, mind, and soul: "Om Mane Padme Hum" (the jewel is in the heart of the lotus). This means that the greatest treasure lies within us; all that we desire and all that we need to know is there. Connecting with God and His angels, and all the blessings of that connection, can be accomplished through meditation. This mantra, "Om Mane Padme Hum," should be repeated silently from this point in meditation onward.

Now visualize the beam of white light continuing upward to the top of your head. This is known as the seventh, or "crown," chakra. Feel and see the entire top of your head filled with bright light. Continue to chant silently, "Om Mane Padme Hum."

If your mind wanders, breathe deeply and listen to the sound of your breath. Relax completely.

Enjoy this state of relaxation as long as possible. You might experience a spiraling sensation, or you might feel dizzy and warm. Any dizziness or spiraling feelings are usually a result of the "rising of Kundalini," which is the psychic power usually dormant at the base of the spine. When it is released, it generally boosts your psychic abilities and creative talents tremendously, and angel communication becomes quite easy. The safest, best method of releasing Kundalini is this technique: slow, controlled meditation with white light.

The final step of this meditation is to see the white beam of light continue upward from the top of your head back out and up into the heavens. See it radiating outward from all parts of your own body and force field. Know that you are projecting light, love, and harmony. Know that other people will sense your harmonious energy and love.

Know that you send out only the best. Know that you will receive back from the universe, and from other human beings, only the best.

This meditation technique might be most effective if someone were to read it to you, since your eyes should be closed. Or you can prerecord an audiotape of yourself reading it aloud.

You should find that this technique clears the path for you to communicate powerfully with the angels. It will help you to disperse the heaviness that may be around you from the weight of your personal problems. You will become a clearer and brighter channel of angel communication. You will become more self-realized—more aware of who you are and why you are here. You may know things about other people that you have no logical way of knowing. You *will* know the joy of being open to God and His angels.

When you are in a meditative state, you may eventually become quite telepathic—able to communicate mentally with others. You may be able to go beyond time and space; the beauty of meditation is that it takes away all limitations. You may even experience a feeling of "electricity" emanating from your head, hands, feet, and, especially, spine . . . particularly just before angelic contact.

You may also experience absolutely nothing. Don't let an absence of experience keep you from meditating, however. Many people have had sudden breakthroughs just when they became discouraged and were about to give up.

Meditation requires dedication and discipline. It can't effectively be done offhandedly or without commitment.

Never stop meditating. Your angel awareness will increase in amazing ways if you commit yourself to meditating fifteen minutes twice a day. You may be able to receive any information you require while you build mental muscle through meditation. For example, if your angelic channel is open as a result of meditation, you will be able to find lost objects. The more you practice, the easier it will be. Many of my radio listeners have called in to my show over the years to ask where their keys or some valuable jewelry might be. Many have asked about lost animals. All of the answers to such questions may be available to you as a result of meditation.

One of my radio listeners called me on the air and asked me where her dad was. She said he had Alzheimer's disease, and had no identification on him. After a few moments of tuning in, I told her I felt that he was in Florida. Strangely enough, though, I did not see palm trees or feel that his setting was tropical. I also told her that he would be found in a place of transportation, such as a train or bus terminal.

After hanging up, my listener told her husband what I had said. He reminded her that her dad had old friends in an upstate New York town called Florida!

They jumped in their car and drove to the town. My listener

remembered what I'd said about "a place that had to do with transportation"; they found her dad sitting on a bench in the bus terminal. Sometimes we just get part of the puzzle, and the rest has to be filled in with our ingenuity and imagination. You see, meditation helps us to use portions of the brain that may otherwise remain unused.

In addition to these benefits, you will find that when you meditate, you have less stress in your life, heightened awareness of all of your senses, and an increased ability to focus and express your creativity.

I also suggest that you write down your angelic requests on white, unlined paper. Write from the heart, clearly and with faith. Writing your thoughts, needs, and desires will help you to focus and energize your requests.

As you are writing, know that your request is being heard by God's messengers. When you are finished, close your eyes and try to visualize what you desire. Use the power of your imagination to see as clearly as possible your wish or need.

The longer you can hold this visualization—even if only for a few seconds—the more angelic strength and power you will add to your communication.

Attitude

Angels love laughter. Joyful energy is so light and airy. Angels will come to you in emergencies, but because "like attracts like," they will also come if they hear laughter. Remember the old saying, "Angels can fly because they take themselves lightly!"

We have learned, too, that nothing heals like laughter. I believe this is because angels love to heal and uplift in an atmosphere of joy, rather than one of gloom. Many people have been healed when humor was abundant. For example, when Norman Cousins, the writer, had a terminal illness, he and his immune system got a tremendous boost from laughter. He watched the funniest videotapes he could find almost around the clock, until he started to heal. Within weeks, he was completely better.

When a dear friend of mine was dying, I made a difficult decision. Once I knew that everything was being done for him, and that he was being well cared for in a hospital, I bought some very funny joke books, including one by Soupy Sales. I called my friend every day and told him, "Get ready to laugh. Even if you don't feel like it." Usually he said, "This is one day that you won't be able to tickle my funny bone. I'm in too much pain."

Undaunted, I gave him my funniest jokes of the day. It never failed; I always heard him laugh. Even if some of them were old and corny, I know they made him feel a bit better.

This does not mean that angels do not respond to other deep emotions, such as grief or great sadness. They do! If you call on your angels in such times, especially using one of the mantras in this book, you should feel their presence. They may help lift your spirits immediately, and much of your sadness can be lessened; or they might wait until you fall asleep, when you may feel what the Bible calls "the peace that passes all understanding."

In addition, it's vital to keep thinking positively. The highest angels in God's universe are attracted to the highest energy. Know in your heart . . . believe in your mind . . . let it flow into your speech and actions that you *know* angels are working with you!

A Powerful Angelic Atmosphere

Angels are attracted to powerful altars. An altar does not have to be in a church; it can be merely a private, spiritual area. If you wish to create one, choose a corner of a room, since corners contain the most powerful energy. Ideally, use a small table covered by a white cloth, and place spiritual pictures, perhaps of Jesus or Moses, photos of departed loved ones, and sketches of angels. Leave open a spiritual book, such as the Kabbalah, Bible, or Bhagavad Gita. Include a bowl of water, since water is a great conductor of spiritual energy (pour out the water after your angelic sessions to dispel any negative energy). Finally, place spiritual artifacts, such as talismans, religious medals, and relics on the altar.

Should space or privacy be an issue, choose a private spot to be your place of angelic contact. Tape a sacred picture on the wall or place it directly in front of you. Meditate on it for a few minutes before you begin any angelic communications.

Add a white candle in a sturdy, fireproof holder. White is the highest vibration color and will draw to you the highest energy. With certain mantras, however, I also recommend the burning of another colored candle as well: green for healing mantras; pink for love mantras; red for spirit contact (use with caution); purple for protection, clairvoyance, and clairaudience mantras; and yellow for mental clarity. Be sure to have a snuffer and a holder for used matches nearby.

Place your written request on this altar, in front of the pictures or sketches. If you like, add fresh white flowers in a vase.

Angels also love bells, chimes, or anything that rings with a beautiful or pleasant sound. The delicate tones of a small handheld bell or even the gentle tinkling of the bell on a cat's collar can attract angels. Hang wind chimes somewhere near the altar; angel wind chimes would be perfect, as would those featuring any symbol of good fortune. I have wind chimes in the shapes of elephants with upturned trunks. In India this is a powerful symbol of good luck.

The ancient Chinese art of Feng Shui (pronounced fung shway) is the study of placement. The Chinese believe that the position of certain objects in a room or building has a tremendous effect on success and happiness. The *chi,* or energy, must thus be nurtured for maximum good fortune. As an example, wind chimes help to keep good luck or *chi* at top levels in a home; aquariums, fountains, or moving water in a room will also bring good fortune and the help of the angels. There are many books on Feng Shui that you can read if you are interested in incorporating this into your angelic atmosphere.

Angel-Attracting Materials

Aromatherapy essential oils, incense, Native American smudge sticks, herbs, and Bach Flower Remedies are among the highest-vibration substances found on the Earth. They are all helpful in your efforts to solidify angelic contact.

Aromatherapy fragrances and essential oils can reliably raise a person's or a room's energy. And all religions recognize that incense or Native American smudge sticks can rid the atmosphere of unwanted negative energy and can also draw positive energy to us.

There are over 350 medicinal plants used for aromatherapy. The secret is to know the purpose of each fragrance and whether it should be used alone or blended with others. Some essential oils should be used in scent diffusers; others may be massaged into the skin, used in the bath or sauna, or used with inhalers.

In the early 1930s, the renowned British physician and scientist Dr. Edward Bach recognized that many of his patients' ills seemed to be related to their various negative states of mind. For example, he noted that anxiety, worrisome thoughts, and even lack of self-confidence so depleted a patient that the body lost its vitality.

He created thirty-eight inexpensive Bach Flower Remedies (found in health food stores and pharmacies). These flower essences work on the delicate but powerful human vibration—which is why angelic energy responds so well to them. All Bach remedies are free of artificial additives and contain the essence of the flower in a small percentage of alcohol to prevent spoilage. They are extremely useful for encouraging angel communication. Read the directions carefully. (Please note: If your local health food store does not carry the Bach Flower Remedies, you may order them by calling 800-334-0843.)

Herbs also facilitate angelic contact. They can be taken as capsules; they can also be effective in an herb pillow or sack. Whether you purchase it or make it, the sack can be filled with herbs then carried on your body or placed under your pillow.

Crystals and Gems

Crystals, like all matter, are made up of atoms, which are in turn composed of electrons, neutrons, and protons. Each of these units of energy contains vibrations, which are the building blocks of all spiritual and physical energy. Many celebrities recognize the benefits of using crystals. Liz Taylor, Oprah Winfrey, and Johnny Carson have been known to use crystals to lift their spirits and to relieve stress. Cybill Shepherd uses crystals for meditation. Anyone can use crystals for healing, to encourage fertility, and to improve memory.

The energy of crystals can help you contact angels. When buying a crystal, choose one that "calls" out to you. Cleanse it first by placing it in salt on a sunny windowsill for two days. You can also run it through a tape demagnetizer, or let the smoke from incense or a smudge stick clear it. Whenever the crystal looks cloudy, it has done its job and will need to be cleansed. Keep your crystals clean and clear, and they will work wonders for you.

Each crystal will have to be programmed by you for its greatest effectiveness. Hold it in your left hand and clearly tell it aloud what you would like it to do for you; then breathe on it three times. Remember to always say "please" and "thank you." You might feel foolish until you realize that the whole system is working!

Additional Suggestions

Read and study literature that deals with angels. Check the RELIGION and NEW AGE sections of your local bookstore. Become an angel expert! Frame and display artwork of angels. Decorate a room, even if it's a bathroom, with an angel motif.

Angels are incredibly subtle. Very few people really "see" angels or clearly "hear" their voices. Contact is often very gentle and easily missed. It can be as delicate as a light breeze against your cheek. Angels are beings of light, without ego, and usually without personalities or names, so don't ask for a name, because you probably won't get it.

Angels should not be confused with spirit guides, master teachers, saints, or deceased relatives. What is the difference between angels and spirit loved ones and teachers? The energy of angels is much higher, clearer, and purer; what they lack in earthly experience they make up for with God's power. Spirit teachers, guides, and deceased loved ones and friends interact with us in more of an "earthy," practical manner than angels.

Always express gratitude. Even a simple, heartfelt "thank you" is enough.

Frequently Asked Questions

If angels are there to protect and guide us, why do accidents and terrible things happen? Angels will come when they are needed, and if they're called. If it seems that angelic protection was not given, it may be that a lesson from God had to be experienced. This is a working out of karma, or destiny.

How do we know when angels are around us, if they're invisible? Angelic energy is delicate and subtle, and can be easily missed. It may be as faint as the sound of a distant brook or a sudden, unexplained trembling or rustling of leaves. Sometimes blades of grass will bend when there's nothing physical to cause it. There can be ripples in water without any disturbance; chills or gooseflesh when we are not cold; tickling sensations anywhere on our bodies or in our hair; the sound of singing or music when no one is around. Also, we might smell flowers or beautiful fragrances with no obvious source, or perhaps an animal or bird will approach us with a loving attitude. Often, an unexplainable feeling of peace, joy, and tranquillity comes over us, particularly in times of sadness, stress, or trauma. Or we might laugh or feel euphoric for absolutely no reason at all! We just have to pay attention.

When can angels most easily be contacted? The strongest angel activity is connected with the cycles of the Earth, at dawn and dusk. These are also the best times for meditation. Other good times are at noon and midnight.

Seasonal changes are also powerfully angelic. In addition, thunderstorms, times of gentle rain, or during a snowfall are good for angel contact. Remember, water conducts spirit energy. I often experience powerful angelic contact while running water in my bathroom; while brushing my teeth or showering, for example.

Where are the best places for angelic contact? Primarily, at places where there is moving water; in natural settings such as forests and glades; in the mountains; at places where streams and bodies of water divide; at forks in roads; and at accident sites. Indoors, try the corners of rooms; thresholds; or where there are people who are about to pass away. Angels also love to be near joyful singing, laughter, celebrations, joy, and newborn babies.

Many people feel the presence of angels while swimming with dolphins, or when attending houses of worship and shrines. There are many places of power on the Earth, or "vortexes," where the energy is extraordinarily elevated. Some of these sacred spots are Sedona, Arizona; Garabandal, Spain; Lourdes, France; Mount Shasta, California; Machu Picchu, Peru; and Medjugorie, Yugoslavia.

What's a quick, easy hint for contacting angels? If you have a small bell, ring it a couple of times. Angels love to hear the sound of bells, and it always gets their attention quickly.

What else? Here's something really amazing. If you have a seashell or a disconnected telephone, hold it up to your ear. Ask your angels, either silently or aloud, to communicate with you.

At first you may hear nothing; it may take time and effort. If you are lucky, you'll be rewarded on your first attempt. Eventually, though, you may hear something: perhaps only a very high, barely perceptible beep or two; or perhaps the sound of rolling thunder, the hum of bees, or actual words. If you cannot understand what you hear, express this in words. Ask that the messages be brought to your correct auditory level. It's all a matter of adjustment and fine-tuning. The point is, if you're calling angels, they will answer you.

Why do we need angels, anyway? Aren't we complete in and of ourselves? I think that this planet and our earthly incarnations are too challenging for us to go from birth to death alone. Angels give us an extra edge— an additional view, from a new perspective. They are always with us. Angels can be as subtle as a fleeting thought, inspiration, or hunch, or as spectacular as a full-bodied materialization when it is needed.

Because the Earth is a difficult place to exist, angels are with us from the moment we take our first breath right up to the moment we take our last. They are with us between lifetimes as well. They go with us from lifetime to lifetime. They know everything about us, and they love us anyway!

What do you think is the most important secret when attempting angel contact? My answer to this comes from one of the greatest teachers who has ever been on the Earth, Paramahansa Yogananda. He said, "If you keep your mind on the resolve to never lose your peace, then you can attain Godliness. Keep a secret chamber of silence within yourself, where you will not let moods, trials, battles, or disharmony enter. Keep out all hatred, revengefulness, and desires. In this chamber of peace, God and His angels will visit you." (From the Self-Realization Teachings of the Paramahansa Yogananda Self-Realization Fellowship, founded in 1920.)

2

Angelic Communication

ow do you know when you are experiencing success-ful angelic communication? In *A Book of Angels,* angel specialist Sophy Burnham tells us that there are three ways of knowing that an angel has come to call: "The angel brings a calm and peaceful serenity that descends sweetly over you, even when the angel is not seen. Their mes-sage is always, 'Fear not! Don't worry.' They say, 'Things are working out perfectly. You're going to like this. Just be patient.' Never once do you hear an angel trumpeting bad news. You remember what you've seen and felt [during the communication], and you are never quite the same again. Angels come in all sizes, shapes, and colors, visible and invisible to the naked eye. But always you are changed from having seen one."

Terry Lynn Taylor, author of several angel books, says in *Messengers of Light,* "Angels speak to us through our thoughts. They will deliver messages in ways we don't expect. They have many ways of reaching us, but often we can miss them."

Pay attention. The message can be as subtle as a bird coming unusually close to you, or as obvious as a car's bumper sticker. Angels frequently communicate through dreams, especially those that you have closest to when you awaken. Because angels often speak through "universal symbology," try to understand your dreams and visions. For example, the word *sink* in a dream could mean a household sink, or possibly "to sink and fall." Angels have a great sense of humor and love to play with words during our dream state. Keep a record of your dreams; much information about your life will be revealed.

Angels will respond if you need inspiration or assistance with a project. Just call out and say that you need help. An angel who is an expert in whatever you are doing should soon be at your side . . . guiding, inspiring, and showing the way.

Here are some of my personal experiences with angels.

Angels Answer My Prayers With an Incredible Vision

Eighteen years ago, I was lost and confused about my career path. Since I wanted to find out the purpose of my life, I chose to enter into a period of prayer and fasting until I had an answer.

It was difficult, since my husband and children still expected to have three meals a day and a neat house, and I also taught yoga classes.

I began each day with a series of prayers asking God and His angels to show me the way. I continued my prayers throughout the day and into the night, asking for clear-cut guidance and information about the purpose of this incarnation. I repeated the words that Edgar Cayce had recommended: "Lord, what wouldst thou have me do?" I drank only water and fruit juice, and ate nothing, since I believe that fasting brings us closer to God. (If you are considering fasting, though, please check with your doctor first.) Of course, my family was concerned and uneasy to see me pass up meals when they were well fed.

On the morning of the tenth day, my angels awakened me at dawn. It sounded like they were singing over my head! When I sat up, I was amazed: It seemed as if my bedroom had become a television studio. I could see the lights hanging from the ceiling, the television cameras, the mike booms—everything.

An angel spoke to me. "Joyce, your destiny is to succeed in television. You are a Light Bearer. Remember three words: *psychic, astrology,* and *yoga.* You will bring all three to the media. Remember this message by using the first three letters of each word: *P, A,* and *Y. P.A.Y.!*"

I went back to sleep. When I awakened a couple of hours later, all was back to normal. In the following weeks, I was in a state of excitement and anticipation, repeating "P. . . . A. . . . . Y. . . ." and wondering how my vision would come true. I had never even been near a television studio.

Then out of the blue, I received a call from a major New York City television station asking me to do a yoga demonstration! After this came another appearance, and another. A television station came on the air near my home, and asked me to do a daily fitness show. I was off and rolling, bitten by the TV bug. Over the years since then, I've had many television appearances, as well as my own shows, almost always about yoga, astrology, and psychicism. My angels certainly were good for their word. Remember the words from the Bible: "Ask and it shall be opened unto you . . . ask with simple faith in your heart."

Angelic Warnings Are Not Always Easy to Understand

Sometimes angels try to warn us about upcoming threats or dangers. Unfortunately, it's not always easy to understand their message or prevent the event from occurring.

One night, I was startled out of a sound sleep. When I opened my eyes, I was blinded by a white light that seemed to fill every corner of the room. As my eyes adjusted to the brightness, I was able to make out what looked like the outline of an angel. I was not at all frightened; as a matter of fact, I went immediately back to sleep. But later that night, I had a most horrific nightmare: Rats were coming at me from a wall, tearing open my face. I saw myself losing blood. This time I woke up screaming and crying. My husband, Jack, reassured me that it was only a dream, and I eventually went back to sleep.

I awoke to a beautiful August day, refreshed but extremely troubled. I did not understand the angelic visitation nor the vivid dream. Was it a warning? If so, what was the message? I tried to meditate to find the answer. I asked God to help me to understand, but came up blank.

Around noon, my brother, Joseph, called me and suggested that our families all pile into his car for a trip out to the Hamptons. It was a glorious day, and we couldn't resist this invitation—even though I was troubled and truly did not wish to leave the house. Within a few minutes, Joe was blowing his car's horn, and we were on our way to Southampton.

Cooper's Beach was clean, the ocean was majestic, and I started to relax, happy that we had agreed to the outing. At about 6 P.M., the seven of us were ambling along the beach, the sun shining directly in our eyes. It was almost impossible to see where we were going. We were walking in the shade of a beach wall.

All of a sudden, I felt a sharp, searing pain on the right side of my face. My family looked at me in horror, and my niece screamed. Looking down, I saw a great deal of blood on my legs. I realized that my face was oozing blood. I remembered my angelic visitation and dream.

Apparently, I had walked into a rusty, razorlike projection that had peeled away from the beach wall. My face was sliced completely open. As my husband tried to stop the bleeding with a beach towel, I clearly heard the voice of an angel saying, "Joyce, be calm. All will be well. You will go through this, and all will be fine. Stay calm. All will be well. Have faith."

A great feeling of peace came to me and stayed, as we walked back to the car, then drove to Southampton Hospital. Because it was Sunday night, there was no surgeon on duty. We called ahead to my local hospital and arranged to be met there by a plastic surgeon. Even though I had lost a great deal of blood, the words of my angel kept resounding in my head: "Stay calm . . . all will be well. Have faith!"

As the surgeon was sewing up my face, he said, "Joyce, I understand you host a television show. Is that correct?"

I told him that I hosted a daily fitness show.

He was quiet for a few minutes while reconstructing my face, then said, "I don't know how to say this, but I don't think you will ever be able to be on television again. The entire right side of your face will be badly scarred, even if you have repeated plastic surgery. This is a very serious injury."

I heard him speaking . . . but I also remembered the words of the angel: "All will be well. Have faith."

In the years that followed, I had many surgical reconstructive procedures. I never stayed away from the opportunity to be on television. Many appearances were extremely difficult; on many programs over the course of many months I had a large bandage on my face. When my face was healing, such as on the *Oprah Winfrey Show,* I had to keep the right side of it away from the camera. Of course, there were also many times when television was out of the question, because my face was simply too inflamed from a surgical procedure for me to appear in public. My television career, which had just started to take off, was definitely dealt a serious blow.

It would have been very easy for me to go into hiding and never appear in public again, especially not on television. There is nothing more critical than the lens of a TV camera. The second most critical thing is a TV producer! They don't miss anything. Many producers criticized the way I tried to face away from the camera, or tried to change the way I sat. I never argued; I just did the best I could. It was never easy. Even dealing with television makeup artists was difficult, because my face was always a challenge to them.

Still, injuring my face only made me stronger. I started to feel that there wasn't anything that could stop me. I was a frequent guest on the shows of Regis Philbin, Sally Jessy Raphael, Oprah Winfrey, Joan Rivers, Phil Donahue, Geraldo Rivera, Soupy Sales, and Merv Griffin; I also appeared on *Entertainment Tonight* and many others, in addition to continuing to host my own show for over fifteen years. I didn't always like the way my face looked, but I wasn't going to let it stop me, either. I felt that I had a job to do.

I just made up my mind that nothing would keep me away from television. I loved being on TV and felt that it was an important part of my destiny. I knew in my heart that my facial injury was one enormous test of my courage, strength, and faith in our Creator and His angels.

I Receive the Gift of a Photograph of an Angel

One of my favorite angel encounters occurred about ten years ago. I decided that I absolutely had to see one of my highest angels. I asked in prayer, over and over again, for the privilege of seeing an angel very clearly. I was adamant. I didn't waver for a moment. I asked before I went to sleep and the first thing when I awoke in the morning. I asked throughout the day. My prayers were relentless. I had to see one of God's messengers.

Finally, a wonderful thing happened. While I was meditating one summer day, a beautiful angel named Mataji came to me. She told me that she came to the Earth to nurture and mother those people who called her. She had long dark hair, huge, luminous brown eyes, and rather full lips. I was struck by the fact that she looked, I thought, very much like me! When she spoke, it sounded like music.

"Joyce, my child, I have heard your call. I will make you a

promise. As a special gift to you, you will have my photograph within twenty-four hours. I will also continue to help you with your psychic readings. Know that I love you now, and have always loved you."

I came out of meditation awe-struck and ecstatic. Then it hit me—a photo? How would that be possible?

Later that day my husband and I were relaxing in our yard. All of a sudden, we looked at each other and almost in unison said, "Let's go to Silver Belle!" Silver Belle was a well-known psychic center in Ephrata, Pennsylvania. People came from all over the world to experience amazing paranormal events. It specialized in séances and psychic readings where you could actually speak to and, in some cases, even see your angels and spirit teachers.

Before we knew it, we had driven the three hours to Silver Belle. The receptionist informed us of the available activities. A new psychic event was being offered that day for the first time: "silk precipitation." Through the talent of a medium, spirit photographs would manifest on silk. Without a moment's hesitation, we paid the admission fee of eight dollars each.

As we entered the séance room, we were greeted with a hug and a loving smile by the trance medium, Joan Donnelly. Six of us were sitting in her circle, and Joan gave us each a piece of white bridal silk and a piece of construction paper. There was a pile of crayons, ink, and paint in the center of the floor. The lights were dimmed, and the séance began. Joan channeled many spirit guides, teachers, and angels. The names and messages given to each of us seemed very accurate and inspiring. While Joan was delivering messages, there was a very strong smell, much like an artist's studio.

When the séance was over, Joan told us to roll the bridal silk up into the construction paper, put a rubber band around it, and open it about an hour later. Since we could not see what was contained within the rolled-up package, the excitement was overwhelming. Finally, one hour later, we opened our construction paper and silk—and guess what! There on my piece of bridal silk was a large, beautiful, clear picture of my angel Mataji.

She looked exactly as I had seen her in my meditation a few hours earlier. Mataji kept her promise, and I had the photo in my hands as proof!

photo credit: Jack Keller

3

Angel Mantras

hese mantras address problems and concerns that affect everyone. Humans all want the same things, and the mantras are divided into categories for ease of finding the one that fits your particular situation. Each mantra includes recommendations that follow the seven methods for opening yourself to angelic assistance discussed in the first chapter. Following these instructions as completely as you can will aid you in your request.

Basic, All-Purpose Mantra

I feel that a basic, all-purpose mantra is "Show me the way, Lord."

Angelic Contact and Protection

For Clairvoyant Angel Contact

ESP Angel, by my fingertips
I feel your touch on my eyes and lips;
Come even closer, let me see
Your brilliance in God's majesty.

Recommendations to help you see your highest angels:

PRAYER   Ask in prayer that you will be able to clearly "see" (clairvoyantly or physically) and communicate with your highest angels.

MANTRA   Use this mantra at least three times a day.

MEDITATION   Sit in a quiet, private place. Listen to the sound of your breath. Meditate on this thought from the Bible: "Ask with the faith of a mustard seed, and it will be given to you."

ATTITUDE   Know in your heart that at the right time, and with God's grace, you will see angels.

ATMOSPHERE   At your altar, ring a bell a few times before starting. Burn a Native American smudge stick.

SUBSTANCES   Make an herbal potpourri containing the Chinese herb alisma, cinnamon, nutmeg, and allspice. Use red rose and angelica aromatherapy oils on your Third Eye, in the center of your forehead.

CRYSTALS & GEMS   Wear or hold a clear quartz, amethyst, moldavite, azurite, green tourmaline, or fluorite crystal.

I can pretty much guarantee you that if you use this mantra and sincerely ask to see an angel, it will happen for you.

For Clairaudient Angel Contact

Messenger of Light
I know you are near
Please open my ears
Your voice let me hear!

Recommendations to help you hear your highest angels:

PRAYER   Ask in prayer to be able to hear your highest angels.

MANTRA   Use this mantra at least three times a day.

MEDITATION   Meditate on the thought, "I know in my heart that it will be for my greatest good to be able to hear my highest angels. It will be a wonderful part of my spiritual growth."

ATTITUDE   Know in your heart that you will be able to hear your angels—faintly at first, then more clearly.

ATMOSPHERE   At your altar, ring a bell a few times before beginning. Burn frankincense incense.

SUBSTANCES   Use any of the following aromatherapy oils on your body: angelica, cypress, and red rose.

CRYSTALS & GEMS   Meditate with clear quartz, amethyst, alexandrite, or moldavite crystals.

For Protection

Guardian Angel
Protect me [or person's name] with your might
Whether waking or sleeping
Both day and night.

Recommendations for increased angelic protection:

PRAYER   When requesting protection for yourself or others, say each person's name aloud, if possible.

MANTRA   Use this mantra before prayers.

MEDITATION   Visualize beams of white light coming down from angelic realms, surrounding and permeating all those for whom you are requesting protection.

ATTITUDE   Your attitude should be one of thankfulness for the requested protection.

ATMOSPHERE   Burn patchouli or frankincense incense, for uplift.

SUBSTANCES   To increase angelic protection, use walnut Bach Flower Remedy, as well as angelica, cassis, and sunlily aromas.

CRYSTALS & GEMS   Wear the crystals fluorite or moldavite, or any religious symbol.

Two Examples of Angelic Protection

A few years ago I was stopped in my car at an intersection that I had gone through many times before. This time was very different, however.

When the light turned green, I tried to step on the gas, but nothing happened. It was as if I couldn't push down on the gas pedal. A little voice in my head said, "Wait, Joyce . . . don't go yet."

So I sat there, even though the light was green, I was in a hurry, and the cars behind me were blowing their horns.

Suddenly, from the road to the right, I saw a huge gas truck barreling through the intersection, intending to go through the red light!

I realized why I had been told to wait by my wonderful angels. When I caught my breath, I thanked them very sincerely.

My mother was physically handicapped, and used a brace and crutches for most of her life. She told me about an incident when she and my dad were coming out of a restaurant. As she attempted to maneuver down the outside steps, she slipped and started to fall. But while she fell, a man appeared out of nowhere, grabbed her under the arms, gently guided her down the steps, and kept her upright. When she and my dad attempted to thank him, they looked around—and he was nowhere in sight. As a matter of fact, there were no people around at all.

For Clearing and Exorcism

Angels of Protection
Angels who Clear
Remove all spirits
Who don't belong here!

When nonphysical entities have not gone into the Light or moved on to higher realms, they often attach themselves to people or places on the Earth. For the greater good of all, angels can be called upon to clear and exorcise these energy forms. Angels will also clean and lift the surrounding physical areas. Virtually all religions practice exorcism rites. Exorcism and clearing usually bring people greater well-being, health, and prosperity.

Recommendations for clearing and exorcism:

PRAYER Ask in prayer for the universe's most powerful, highest angels to come in and rid the environment of all entities who are not there "in God's name."

MANTRA Shout this mantra as loud as you can, many times, until you feel that the atmosphere is clear. Combine it with formal prayers that you know if you feel there is still unwanted energy. Use the names of your highest teachers if you know them, sacred names, or just call on God.

MEDITATION   In meditation, try to know that your atmosphere is being cleared and uplifted.

ATTITUDE   Have an attitude of power and strength. Do not express fear. Know that God's highest angels are with you.

ATMOSPHERE   Get holy water from the vestibule of any Catholic church—and please put a dollar or two, or whatever you can afford, into the donation box. Put the water into a spray bottle and spray all areas that need cleansing, particularly the corners of each room. Use this mantra along with prayer, as you spray. Sprinkle kosher salt into each corner. Place a bowl of water containing a piece of camphor under your bed. Change the water and camphor weekly; do not let your pets drink this.

SUBSTANCES   Burn sage incense and a large white candle. Have a glass of water to attract negativity. Pour it down the toilet when you are finished cleansing the rooms.

CRYSTALS & GEMS   Wear jewelry that is sacred to you when performing clearing and cleansing. Carry a black obsidian crystal.

For the Protection of Children

Angels who Protect Wee Ones
Watch, protect, guide
Please never leave
Or go from this child's side!

Recommendations for the protection of children:

PRAYER   Ask for a child's protection in prayer. Use his full name; say it aloud.

MANTRA   Repeat this mantra each time you request protection.

MEDITATION   Visualize four powerful angels surrounding and protecting the child.

ATTITUDE   Teach the child a simple prayer of angelic protection that is in keeping with your religious beliefs.

ATMOSPHERE   Make sure your home is filled with love and the highest, most positive energy. When you meditate, burn patchouli or frankincense incense. Place a religious symbol over the child's bed.

SUBSTANCES   Use jasmine or geranium aromatherapy fragrances in your home, and on your body.

CRYSTALS & GEMS   Carry a clear quartz crystal with you, and use one for meditation.

For Travel Protection

Dear Angels of Travel
Planes, cars, trains, ships
Give me complete protection
For both long and short trips.

Recommendations for travel protection:

PRAYER   Before getting on a plane, train, ship, or car, ask the angels of travel to surround the conveyance with their full angelic protection, and to bathe it completely in God's white light.

MANTRA   Use this mantra before taking any trips.

MEDITATION   Before or during the travel experience, clearly envision yourself arriving safely at your destination. Actually see yourself walking off the plane or leaving the ship.

ATTITUDE   Your attitude should be one of gratitude for a safe, enjoyable trip.

ATMOSPHERE   Use jasmine and peppermint aromatheraphy body oils.

SUBSTANCES   If you are afraid to travel, Bach Flower Rescue Remedy will usually remove all fear.

CRYSTALS & GEMS   A sugilite crystal helps to bring serenity when traveling because of its great protective qualities. Religious medals are also helpful.

To Bless a Home

Angels of Hearth and Home
Bring blessings, ceilings to floors
Spread your angelic light
For only joy behind these doors.

Recommendations to bless and bring joy to a home:

PRAYER   In your prayers, ask that your home receive God's greatest joys and blessings.

MANTRA   Use this angel mantra as you walk around your home, blessing it. Do this at least once a month.

MEDITATION   In meditation, visualize four angels protecting your home—one in each corner of your property.

ATTITUDE   Your attitude should reflect appreciation for all the blessings that you have received, and that will be forthcoming, in your home.

ATMOSPHERE   Your home's atmosphere should be that of a haven of love. All who enter should feel welcome and nurtured. Use Native American smudge sticks to cleanse your home of any unwanted energy. Spritz your home with holy water or Florida water whenever you wish to raise its angelic energy.

SUBSTANCES   Use white candles on your dinner table as well as on your angel altar to increase your home's blessings. Kosher salt sprinkled into a room's corners while repeating of prayers and the mantra will also increase angel energy.

CRYSTALS & GEMS The crystal black obsidian is wonderful when placed on a coffee table. It will help to absorb negative energy, and keep angelic energy at peak levels.

Angels Protect My Home

I was a teenager, living at home with my parents. At about two in the morning, I was awakened out of a deep sleep by a gentle, firm voice telling me, "Joyce, get up." This continued until I finally got out of bed.

The voice then stated, again firmly, "Joyce, walk to the top of the basement stairs and sniff." Teenagers hate being told what to do, and I was not different. Still, the voice insisted, so I obeyed the instructions.

At first, I didn't smell anything. Then a faint acrid odor wafted from the basement. Fully awake now, I followed the smell downstairs to the oil burner. An oily rag draped on an overhead pipe was beginning to smolder. Quickly, I took down the rag and drenched it, preventing what could have been a very serious fire.

Apparently, when our oil had been delivered earlier that day, the deliverer neglected to clean up all of his rags and left one in this dangerous spot. The angels saved my family and me from this potentially lethal situation.

To Express Gratitude

Heavenly Angels!
Thank you for all!
You helped, you heard
You answered my call!

Recommendations for expressing gratitude:

PRAYER   Express gratitude to the angels in your prayers and acknowledge all that comes your way. This will help you to grow spiritually and will keep the blessings forthcoming. Always finish with, "Thy will be done."

MANTRA   I believe that this angel mantra is the most important of all. Repeat it often; it is an effective way of expressing gratitude.

MEDITATION   Begin your meditation with thoughts of thankfulness and acknowledgment. These will be instantly confirmed by your angels.

ATTITUDE   Be grateful for whatever it is that you have received—even if it is not what you requested!

ATMOSPHERE   Your atmosphere should reflect that gratitude. Place artwork in your home that shows some of the beauty of angels.

SUBSTANCES   Diffuse angelica aromatherapy fragrance oil in your home.

CRYSTALS & GEMS   A clear quartz crystal strategically and attractively placed on an end table is always a nice, appreciative touch.

Knife-Sharpening Angel

Another of my favorite angel encounters occurred on a very hot July day. My husband, Jack, and I had just moved into our first house. Our furniture was to be delivered that afternoon. Before leaving for work that morning, Jack helped me unroll our new carpet. We realized it had to be cut to fit the room before the furniture could be brought in. He gave me a pair of carpet scissors, which he tested for sharpness on the carpet before he left for work.

The scissors did a fairly decent job of cutting the carpet for the first half hour. But as I continued to cut, I realized that there was no way that they would be able to finish the job. They had grown incredibly dull, and were beginning to cause tremendous shooting pains in my thumb and hand. I felt that I was starting to have nerve damage in my hand.

Since I didn't have a car and was miles away from any stores, I started to become quite frantic. Our lack of air-conditioning worsened my profuse perspiration and desperation. I sat on the floor trying to figure out how I could sharpen the scissors. It was quite impossible, since none of our household tools had arrived.

When I was just at the point of giving up, I thought that I heard the gentle tinkling of bells . . . just like the knife-sharpening trucks that occasionally came through my neighborhood in Brooklyn when I was growing up. I chuckled to myself, thinking, "Silly girl. You haven't seen one of those trucks for over twenty years! The jingling must be coming from a Good Humor ice-cream truck. Don't even bother to stand up and look out the window. You'll just be disappointed."

I tried not to look, but after a few more minutes of bell jingling I could no longer resist. I couldn't believe my eyes—outside the window, an old and dirty knife-sharpening truck was slowly driving! I ran out like a wild woman, waving my dull scissors in my hand.

While an elderly gentleman with twinkly eyes sharpened my scissors, it crossed my mind that I probably didn't have any money in the house. When he was finished, though, he asked me for two dollars. Amazingly, that was exactly the amount I had in my wallet. The scissors worked wonderfully well, and I finished cutting the carpet moments before our furniture arrived.

We lived in that house over ten years. I never again saw that strange type of vehicle come through our neighborhood: That dusty old truck with the elderly scissors sharpener was definitely sent by the angels.

Personal Growth

For Strength

Angels of Power
Angels divine
Reverse all weakness
Let strength be mine!

Recommendations for strength:

PRAYER   Pray for increased power. It may not always be quickly or easily discernible, but your strength will increase.

MANTRA   Use this mantra whenever you desire extra strength or power.

MEDITATION   Visualize yourself with a lion superimposed over you; see yourself with the strength of the king of the jungle.

ATTITUDE   Visualize clearly that you are a "tower of strength."

ATMOSPHERE   Create an atmosphere of the greatest power through the use of Feng Shui. Place your bed or desk so that it faces the door. Hang angelic wind chimes over the area where you desire the greatest power.

SUBSTANCES   Use the cherry plum, elm, gorse, larch, cerato, and, especially, aspen Bach Flower Remedies. Peppermint and almond are the aromatheraphy fragrances that bring the greatest power.

CRYSTALS & GEMS   Carnelian and citrine quartz crystals also help empower.

For Overcoming Fear

Angels of Light
Let me feel you are near
Get rid of all fright
Please take away all fear!

Recommendations to help overcome fear:

PRAYER   In your prayers, simply ask for courage to replace fear.

MANTRA   Memorize this mantra, and repeat it for instant and powerful strength.

MEDITATION   Visualize the tallest, most empowering angels standing on either side of you.

ATTITUDE   Know that beautiful, powerful angels of light are clearing the path for you. They surround and permeate you with their strength.

ATMOSPHERE   Bring powerful colors, such as red, into your home; and wear them whenever you need to feel empowered.

SUBSTANCES   The aspen, centaury, cherry plum, cerato, and mimulus Bach Flower Remedies are the most strengthening. Aromatherapy fragrances to use are chamomile and red apple.

CRYSTALS & GEMS   Carry carnelian or sodalite crystals with you.

For Confidence

Angels of Confidence
Angels of Might
Help me walk in power
Knowing my path is right!

Recommendations to gain confidence:

PRAYER   Ask in your prayers for the highest angels to boost your confidence.

MANTRA   Use this mantra whenever you need greater assurance. It will never fail you.

MEDITATION   In meditation, visualize God's most surefooted, confident angels carrying shields and surrounding you. See them clearing the path for you so that you can walk in power!

ATTITUDE   Maintain an attitude as steady and confident as the powerful angels you visualized in your prayers and meditation. See them as clearly as possible to allow them to work with you even more powerfully.

ATMOSPHERE   Create an atmosphere that empowers you, one free of clutter and confusion. Spend a few moments at your altar whenever your confidence needs a boost. If you cannot physically be there, see your altar in your mind's eye.

SUBSTANCES The Bach Flower Remedies that will help your
boost your confidence are aspen, cerato, crab apple, gorse, and, especially
larch. The aromatherapy fragrances that will help you are cypress, peppermint, peach, and jasmine.

CRYSTALS & GEMS Carry carnelian or citrine crystals with you.

For Finding Your Life's Purpose

Angels of Destiny
Angels who light life's way
Help me to see my purpose
To make the most of each day.

Recommendations to help you find your life's work, goals, or purpose:

PRAYER   In your prayers, ask your angels to show you what you wish to know about your life's work, goals, or purpose. Ask until you receive your answer.

MANTRA   Use the mantra whenever you wish to focus your energies.

MEDITATION   Visualize yourself standing on a mountaintop. See yourself first covered completely with clouds. Slowly, see the clouds dissipate. Envision yourself clearly standing in the sunshine, without a hint of cloudiness around you.

ATTITUDE   Develop a "knowingness" about yourself. This meditation will help you.

ATMOSPHERE   Your growth and understanding will be enhanced by peppermint aromatherapy oil.

SUBSTANCES   The use of wild oat and wild rose Bach Flower Remedies will be very helpful in focusing your energies.

CRYSTALS & GEMS   Meditate with clear quartz crystal, smoky quartz, or citrine quartz to assist the work of the angels.

To Increase Humility

Angels of Ego
Angels so humble
Bring me more balance
Don't let me stumble.

Recommendations of ways to increase humility and decrease ego:

PRAYER   In your prayers, ask your angels to teach you while awake and asleep. Ask them if lack of humility is retarding the growth of your soul.

MANTRA   Repeat this mantra twice whenever you feel that your ego is out of control.

MEDITATION   In your meditation, ask your angels to show you the extent of their humility. Ask them to demonstrate the ways that humility increases power, and how it can work best for you.

ATTITUDE   Your attitude should be one of receptivity and understanding. Know in your heart that your humility is the key to your soul's greatest growth.

ATMOSPHERE   Burning Native American smudge sticks or myrrh will help to create the perfect atmosphere for angelic assistance.

SUBSTANCES   The Bach Flower Remedies beech, vervain, vine, and water violet will all be helpful to you.

CRYSTALS & GEMS   Use an amethyst for meditation, to keep your energies harmonized.

For Tolerance

Angels of Forbearance
Bring mercy and grace
Remove all intolerance
Leave not a trace.

Recommendations to help increase tolerance:

PRAYER Pray and your level of tolerance will increase.

MANTRA Repeat this mantra when you need tolerance. You will feel your angels draw close to you.

MEDITATION Reflect on great leaders and teachers from history; Mother Teresa, for example. Ask your angels to help fill you with the mercy of these people.

ATTITUDE Your attitude should be nonjudgmental and noncritical. Be aware of your speech. Stop yourself short when you hear or before you speak words of criticism or judgment.

ATMOSPHERE Be welcoming to all, without any of the barriers that discriminate or divide us as human beings.

SUBSTANCES When your tolerance needs a boost, rely on the beech, heather, and impatiens Bach Flower Remedies.

CRYSTALS & GEMS Carry the crystal kunzite, which is also known as pink spodumene, with you.

For Creativity

Angels of Creativity
Let inspiration grow
Please touch my head
Let my creativity flow!

Recommendations for increased creativity:

PRAYER   Pray for increased creativity. This should help jump-start your energies.

MANTRA   Repeat this mantra, when you need creativity, over flowing water (a sink is fine). It will work wonders.

MEDITATION   Visualize the angels of creativity pouring ideas and inspiration into your head. Visualize this image repeatedly, until you have more creative energy than you can handle.

ATTITUDE   Pay attention to even the smallest spark of creativity. Sometimes inspiration is so subtle that it can hardly be perceived.

ATMOSPHERE   Use jasmine aromatherapy oil. Ring a little bell whenever you wish to call for help from the angels.

SUBSTANCES   Angel-attracting substances that will increase creativity are the Bach Flower Remedies clematis and olive.

CRYSTALS & GEMS   The crystals to have on your body or, as an example, on your computer are citrine and celestite. For increased imagination, use sodalite and kyanite. Red garnets are also conducive to creative energy.

For Spiritual Growth

Angels of Spirituality
Who increase our might
Touch my Third Eye
Fill me with God's light!

Recommendations to help increase spiritual growth:

PRAYER   For the best results, prayers for spiritual growth should be made either outside in a holy place or at the highest altitude available, be it a hill, mountain, or rooftop.

MANTRA   Use this angel mantra throughout the day and before meditation. Be near a body of water—or at least have water nearby.

MEDITATION   Center your meditation on the Third Eye, also known as the eye of God: the area between the eyebrows and about an inch above. When this chakra is open, or "charged," you will experience tremendous spiritual growth, intuition, and understanding. See this chakra filled with white light, which then fills the top of your head and travels outward and upward.

ATTITUDE   Consider eliminating meat and sugar from your diet to encourage spiritual energy.

ATMOSPHERE   Meditate in the same place and at the same time every day. Burn a seven-day white candle on your altar (in a bowl of water for safety reasons) to help attract the highest angelic energy.

SUBSTANCES   Use chestnut bud or chicory Bach Flower Remedy. Carry the Chinese herb alisma, which is usually found in Chinese pharmacies, in a small pouch.

CRYSTALS & GEMS   Use clear quartz crystals, amethyst, moldavite, green tourmaline, or fluorite crystals in meditation. Carry a small black obsidian stone with you. Look at it from time to time.

For Facing Insurmountable Tasks

Angels of Life
Your divine rays guide me
Let me feel your strength
As you walk and stand beside me.

Recommendations for facing insurmountable tasks:

PRAYER   Ask in your prayers for God's invisible helpers to support, help, and guide you through this difficult time.

MANTRA   Use this mantra when you are faced with a challenge and need an extra push. It will work wonders for you!

MEDITATION   Meditate on the thought that you have no limitations. Ignore negative feedback that is dished in your direction. Know that with the help of the angels, you can rise to the greatest heights; insurmountable tasks will not be a problem with your invisible support system.

ATTITUDE   Avoid negative thoughts or words, especially about yourself.

ATMOSPHERE   Based on the openness of Feng Shui, create an expansive atmosphere so your mind is free to soar and to reach your highest potential.

SUBSTANCES   The Bach Flower Remedies aspen, cerato, elm, gorse, larch, and pine will help, as will Neroli aromatherapy oil.

CRYSTALS & GEMS   Carry a black obsidian, which is known for its ability to physically empower and emotionally strengthen. It will reliably assist you and your angels.

For Help With Difficult Decisions

Angels of Resolution
Which way do I go?
Show me the answer
So the decision I'll know!

Through the grace of our Creator, humankind has been given the gift of free will. That means that we, as human beings, always have the last word when it comes to making choices. It also means that angels cannot and will not interfere when a decision has to be made. However, when we ask for their help, they always do the best they can to help us. Therefore, I feel that the angels' answers to our request for help with a decision will be forthcoming, but may be very subtle!

Recommendations for making a difficult decision:

PRAYER   Ask in prayer for the angels' help in making a decision. Listen and watch carefully all that you see and hear after such a request.

MANTRA   Repeat this angel mantra three times before going to bed. It may bring an answer when you awaken.

MEDITATION   In meditation, see yourself holding a large white pad. You may find an answer written on that pad, if you pay close attention.

ATTITUDE   Maintain an attitude that is perceptive and aware.

ATMOSPHERE   Create an atmosphere that is relaxed, comfortable, and receptive.

SUBSTANCES The Bach Flower Remedy scleranthus will help you with a difficult decision.

CRYSTALS & GEMS Carry citrine crystal with you for its problem-solving energy.

To Restore Faith in God

Angels of Faith
I'm lost to the core
Please fill my heart
My faith fully restore.

Recommendations for the restoration of faith in God:

PRAYER   Simply recognizing that there has been a loss of faith is an important step in the path back to God. Your prayers should do just that. Express from your heart that your faith has been shaken, and ask for restoration.

MANTRA   Repeat this angel mantra to allow the angels to work with you to restore your faith.

MEDITATION   In meditation, visualize angels walking and talking with you. You can't quite hear what they tell you, but you know in your heart and mind that you are beginning to experience a restoration of faith.

ATTITUDE   Your attitude may be skeptical, even discouraged or angry. The secret, though, is to let the angels enter your life and touch the soul of your being. This frequently happens while sleeping.

ATMOSPHERE   Use bergamot and agrimony aromatherapy fragrance oils.

SUBSTANCES   Use cerato, gentian, or gorse Bach Flower Remedies.

CRYSTALS & GEMS   Green tourmaline, fluorite, and black obsidian crystals will help you balance and harmonize your energies.

To Increase Energy

Angels of Vitality
Put a lift in my step
I want to be a dynamo
Filled with energy and pep!

Recommendations for increasing energy:

PRAYER   Pray with receptive gratitude for the energy that will be forthcoming.

MANTRA   Repeat this mantra whenever you need an energy boost.

MEDITATION   See yourself with the vitality, energy, and pep of the most active five-year-old you can think of.

ATTITUDE   Expect bursts of energy. Expect to sleep less. Expect to feel energized!

ATMOSPHERE   It will help the angels boost your energy if your atmosphere has as much fresh air and sunlight as possible. Feng Shui tells us that fresh air and light must circulate freely! Get rid of those heavy drapes and shades. Move furniture away from windows. Let the *chi* (energy) flow easily into your home or office. Sleep with a large glass of fresh water near your head. Don't drink it.

SUBSTANCES   The most helpful angelic substances are the Bach Flower Remedies clematis and hornbeam. Herbs that will help energize you are suma, mara, kola nut, echinacea, licorice fo-ti, and rehmannia, and the Chinese fruits cornus and dioscorea.

CRYSTALS & GEMS   Carry a clear quartz crystal to absorb negativity and keep you energized.

For Mental Clarity

Angels of Mentality
Always touching near
Keep my mind sharp
Always quick and clear.

Recommendations for increased mental clarity:

PRAYER   Pray for mental sharpness, clarity, and excellent memory.

MANTRA   Repeat this mantra whenever you wish to clear your mind.

MEDITATION   See a clear quartz crystal hovering over your head. Visualize God's white light coming down in a strong beam. The light goes through the crystal, then down completely through your head and whole body, right down to your toes. It comes up again, carrying all negativity and mental fatigue with it, through your head, out to the crystal, and back up to the universe.

ATTITUDE   Maintain an attitude of knowing that your mind is crystal clear and sharp. This "knowingness" also helps attract angel assistance.

ATMOSPHERE   Keep your atmosphere as free of clutter and confusion as possible.

SUBSTANCES   The Bach Flower Remedy chestnut bud will help you achieve clarity. Mental exhaustion is relieved by the Bach Flower Remedy olive. Marjoram is the aromatherapy oil that helps clear the mind. The herbs that assist are ginkgo biloba, fo-ti, gota kola, and damiana. The most common method of taking herbs is by capsule, but the most potent is usually the tincture. Follow the directions on the label.

CRYSTALS & GEMS   Fluorite and selenite, which is also known as gypsum, carry angel energy that will help with mental clarity.

For Patience and Poise

Angels of Patience
Fill me with poise
Let me rise above
Irritation, clatter and noise.

Recommendations to increase patience and poise:

PRAYER   Pray for serenity and peace.

MANTRA   Repeat this mantra when you feel irritated. It will work wonders in helping you rise above irritations.

MEDITATION   In meditation, see yourself jumping into a pile of white cotton balls; let the cotton support the weight of your body and absorb all noise and irritation.

ATTITUDE   Release and reject all loud or irritating noises or interference.

ATMOSPHERE   A more serene atmosphere may require the installation of acoustical tiles, extra-thick carpeting, or soundproof drapes.

SUBSTANCES   The most uplifting angelic substances are the centaury, mimulus, vervain, and vine Bach Flower Remedies. Use kava-kava and valerian to soothe nerves, and try neroli aromatherapy oil in a diffuser.

CRYSTALS & GEMS   Carry a pink quartz crystal with you to help you create a tranquil atmosphere.

Love

To Find Your Soul Mate

Angel of Love
Angel of Light
Please find my soul mate
No later than tonight!

Recommendations to help you find your soul mate:

PRAYER   Use prayer and visualization to help you find your soul mate.

MANTRA   Use this mantra at least three times a day, especially before leaving your home.

MEDITATION   Imagine clearly what you would like your soul mate to be. Use as much detail as possible.

ATTITUDE   Keep your attitude positive! Let the angels know that you will do everything to help them bring your soul mate to you. Ask them to show you what would be helpful. Love yourself honestly, and love will come to you.

ATMOSPHERE   Create an atmosphere of receptivity. Bring bright colors into your home, especially pink.

SUBSTANCES   Use vanilla and rose aromatherapy oils. Keep nutmeg, cinnamon, and allspice in a small pouch, in your pocket or next to your skin.

CRYSTALS & GEMS   Carry a pink quartz crystal as close to your heart as possible, and remember the power of a smile!

For Love at First Sight

Angel of Love
Angel of Light
Let us experience
Love at first sight!

Recommendations for love at first sight with your soul mate:

PRAYER   Ask simply and with faith for your prayers to be answered.

MANTRA   Recite this mantra throughout the day, and before going to sleep.

MEDITATION   Each time you use the mantra, clearly visualize your ideal soul mate.

ATTITUDE   Have an attitude of positive, loving empowerment.

ATMOSPHERE   Create an atmosphere of loving receptivity on your altar and in your home by burning patchouli or ylang-ylang incense.

SUBSTANCES   Use red rose or cypress aromatherapy oil. This can be inhaled or used as a body oil.

CRYSTALS & GEMS   Wear a hematite crystal to make dreams come true and rose quartz to attract love.

For Faithful Love

Angel of Fidelity!
Create a circle with no end
Ensure faithful love
With my heart's best friend.

Recommendations for ensuring faithful love:

PRAYER   Ask in your prayers for your union to be blessed by the angels.

MANTRA   Recite this mantra three times a day.

MEDITATION   Each time you repeat the mantra, see the two of you together, surrounded by a clear pink shell. Envision the two of you inside that shell, hugging and holding each other. Visualize this eggshell bathed in warm pink light.

ATTITUDE   Your attitude toward your loved one should be one of love, trust, and devotion.

ATMOSPHERE   Your atmosphere should include the understanding and practice of Feng Shui. One way this ancient art can be used to ensure fidelity in a relationship is through small mirrors. Small mirrors should be placed in any windows where you can view sharp corners projecting in the direction of your home from any neighboring roofs or buildings. The idea is to reflect away from your home any negative energy.

SUBSTANCES   Use ylang-ylang, vanilla musk, jasmine, and rose on your body and in your home. These are uplifting, angel-attracting aromas.

CRYSTALS & GEMS   Pink quartz crystals should be placed under your mattress, one under each corner. Both you and your loved one should carry or wear a pink quartz crystal.

For Lasting Love

Angel of Love
Let there be
An overwhelming desire
For [name] to be with me!

Recommendations for lasting love:

PRAYER   In your prayers, envision you and your loved one surrounded by a pink sphere and bathed in a warm pink light.

MANTRA   This mantra should be used at least three times a day.

MEDITATION   In your meditation, see yourself and your loved one surrounded by a bright white light and then a sphere of warm pink light. Practice this visualization technique throughout your relationship.

ATTITUDE   Never falter in your belief that the two of you are destined to be together.

ATMOSPHERE   Place a red seven-day candle in a bowl of water (for safety reasons) at your altar. Let it burn day and night for a week. Use prayer in conjunction with the burning of this candle. Express your heart's desires.

SUBSTANCES   Use ylang-ylang, musk, jasmine, and rose oils, both in your home and as a personal fragrance.

CRYSTALS & GEMS   Smoky quartz (to make dreams come true), jade (for power), and pink quartz crystals will help to attract angelic assistance.

For a Marriage Proposal

Love Angel
Our hearts would sing
If our love was blessed
With a wedding ring!

Recommendations to help you get a marriage proposal:

PRAYER   Ask in your prayers for a blessed marriage, for the greater good of all concerned.

MANTRA   Use this mantra throughout the day, especially in relaxed moments.

MEDITATION   Visualize the two of you standing at the altar exchanging vows. Energize this meditation by seeing a downpouring of white light.

ATTITUDE   Keep your attitude loving and positive, but without pressure, toward your loved one.

ATMOSPHERE   Have a picture of the two of you on your altar. Burn a white seven-day candle next to the photo (in a bowl of water).

SUBSTANCES   Make a fragrant home potpourri that will attract angelic assistance from cinnamon, nutmeg, and allspice. Wear the fragrance ylang-ylang or jasmine.

CRYSTALS & GEMS   Carry a pink quartz crystal (in a white satin pouch) close to your heart.

To Conceive a Baby

Angel of Fertility
Please, a baby girl or boy
To bless our love
And fill our home with joy!

Recommendations to help conceive a baby:

PRAYER   Ask in your prayers for God to bless your union with a child.

MANTRA   Use this mantra throughout the day, especially before attempting conception.

MEDITATION   In meditation, visualize yourself holding your very own sweet little baby. See yourself kissing the fontanel, or "soft spot," on the top of the baby's head.

ATTITUDE   Maintain an attitude of loving encouragement. Let the incoming entity, or baby, know that you and your mate will be loving, nurturing, supportive parents. Send loving thoughts about your child out into the angelic realms.

ATMOSPHERE   Using Feng Shui, make sure your home has living plants and moving water—as with an aquarium, for instance—for maximum angelic energy.

SUBSTANCES   If you have had difficulty conceiving, make sure that both of you have been tested by an endocrinologist for chemical imbalances. Both of you should take vitamin E for fertility. In addition, Oriental dew, rose, and angelica aromas are conducive to conception.

CRYSTALS & GEMS   Carry a jade gemstone or moonstone for fertility. If possible, both you and your mate should tape a small moonstone to your stomachs, directly above the pubic bone. (A moonstone on a belly chain also works.) Wear it both day and night.

To Heal a Broken Heart

Angels of Compassion
Let the healing start!
Please stop the pain
Mend my broken heart.

Recommendations to help heal a broken heart:

PRAYER   In your prayers, ask for help in changing your sad feelings to those of joy.

MANTRA   Use this mantra at least three times a day.

MEDITATION   Visualize your heart chakra completely filled with a blinding pink light. Practice this every day for at least five minutes.

ATTITUDE   Have an attitude receptive to the healing of your emotions. Allow the angels to lift and repair your aura. Cooperate by not clinging to sorrowful memories.

ATMOSPHERE   Do not go where there are sad memories or play sad music. Try something new instead. Assist the angels who are working with you.

SUBSTANCES   The aromatherapy fragrances bergamot, gardenia, tuberose, and freesia rain, homeopathic remedy, Ignatius.

CRYSTALS & GEMS   The crystals to carry with your are obsidian (to help with detachment), smoky crystal, and pink quartz crystal. Wear the quartz crystal close to your heart.

To Ease Unrequited Love

Angels of Love
Who hear our heart's desires
Please bring me
What my soul requires.

Recommendations for help with unrequited love:

PRAYER   In your prayers, ask your angels to show you the path of your heart's greatest joy.

MANTRA   Use the angel mantra whenever you wish to manifest your heart's desires.

MEDITATION   In your meditation, visualize your heart. Surround it completely in warm, loving pink light. Repeat this whenever you wish to move away from your frustrated feelings about your unrequited love.

ATTITUDE   Know that things will get better. Your life will improve. Tell yourself, "This too shall pass."

ATMOSPHERE   Your atmosphere—both your home and clothing—should have bright pink and yellow touches. Burn bergamot, oriental dew, freesia rain, and tuberose aromatherapy oils to attract even more angel assistance.

SUBSTANCES   Use agrimony, crab apple, or gentian Bach Flower Remedies to help you feel immediately better and rise above your emotional pain.

CRYSTALS & GEMS   Carry a pink tourmaline crystal or onyx gemstone with you, to aid detachment.

For Fullfilling and Satisfying Sex

Angels of Passion
With sensuality your tool
Help us heat up
What should no longer be cool!

Recommendations for fulfilling and satisfying sex:

PRAYER   Your prayers and attention should initially focus on the first chakra at the base of the spine. Draw your attention to that chakra, filling it with white light. See that white light get brighter and brighter as it fills the lower half of your body. Then allow it to come slowly up your spine to the top of your head. Ideally, this should be done with your love partner.

MANTRA   Use this angel mantra while holding a photo of the person whom you choose as a partner.

MEDITATION   The best meditation for fulfilling sex is music; play it from the beginning of your time together to help set the tone of love. Then, to arouse passion, play some romantic yet exciting music, like Ravel's *Bolero*. Also consider CDs or tapes of nature sounds, like thunderstorms, rain falling, or a babbling brook.

ATTITUDE   Maintain attitudes that are loving and supportive of one another. Read books together such as *The Art of Sensual Massage,* or *Tantric Massage for Lovers Only*. Practice new techniques with a playful, joyful attitude. Use slippery body oils. Laughter lifts all situations to higher vibratory levels, and always brings in the support of playful cherubs. This will always leave you with a feeling of joie de vivre. Not only will you love life even more, but your love for each other will be expanded!

ATMOSPHERE   Your atmosphere should be cozy and welcoming. Use these aromatherapy oils in your home, on your bodies, or as massage oils: ylang-ylang, almond, and jasmine. Practice Feng Shui to enhance lovemaking: The Chinese tell us that maximum good energy comes when the bed is facing the door of the room.

SUBSTANCES   The following herbs, in capsule or tincture form, often help increase sexuality: fo-ti root, gota kola, and damiana (for women); Panax ginseng, yohimbe, saw palmetto, and aveena sativa (for men). The Chinese herb shizandra, corn silk, and the Amazon rain forest herb muira pauma help both men and women. Use crab apple Bach Flower Remedy.

CRYSTALS & GEMS   For maximum angelic support, place one pink quartz crystal under each corner of your mattress, or on the floor under each corner of your bed. The size of the crystals does not matter. Place a bowl of water under your bed, also. Empty it once a week. Be sure pets cannot drink the water or upset the bowl.

To Improve Relationships With Children

Angels of Parenting
Help keep our bonds strong
Let my dear children
Love me deeply, well and long.

Recommendations to help improve relations with your children:

PRAYER   Ask the angels in prayer for improved relations. Prayers from parents are always the brightest and most powerful, as perceived in angelic realms, especially this type of prayer. Pray for your children while they are sleeping.

MANTRA   Use this mantra in combination with prayer throughout the day, or when you wish to bring your children closer to you.

MEDITATION   See in your mind's eye a very clear picture of you and your children as you looked at your happiest time. Surround that mental photo with God's white light. Do this when you wish to strengthen the bond.

ATTITUDE   Your attitude toward your children should be one of genuine interest and involvement. Let them know that you will always be there for them, and always love them.

ATMOSPHERE   Create an atmosphere at home of loving support. Following Feng Shui, make sure angel energy flows through your home at maximum joyful levels. This may mean placing an aquarium or moving water in your home, along with a number of live plants. Burn incense or a smudge stick in their rooms while they are in school or out of the house.

SUBSTANCES   Use ylang-ylang and red rose aromatherapy oils in a diffuser in your home.

CRYSTALS & GEMS   Carry a pink kunzite crystal for emotional harmony and balance.

Physical and Emotional Help

For Healing

Dear Angel of Healing
You're what is needed
With God's permission
This message is heeded!

Recommendations for healing of the body, mind, and soul:

PRAYER   Ask in prayer for the healing that is needed.

MANTRA   Use this mantra a minimum of three times a day.

MEDITATION   Picture as clearly as possible the person who needs healing. See her bathed in bright white light. Imagine her completely and perfectly well. Try to see angels actually touching and working on her.

ATTITUDE   Know in your heart, mind, and soul that your prayers are heard and will be answered according to God's highest purpose.

ATMOSPHERE   Create a healing atmosphere around the person in need of healing. If he is bedridden, create a small altar next to him.

SUBSTANCES   Make a small pillow containing pine, eucalyptus, bergamot, and red rose olive or sweet chestnut Bach Flower Remedies. Burn a green candle for healing, or use the homeopathic remedy, Ignatius.

CRYSTALS & GEMS   Meditate with clear quartz crystal, tourmaline, or jade.

Powerful Angelic Healing Technique

Anyone with a desire to be used as an instrument of healing can easily do so. The secret of healing is prayer, be it for yourself, another human being, or an animal. If you have the desire or need to heal someone, try the following:

1. Close your eyes. Visualize yourself and the person being healed each surrounded by an egg of protection. This egg is itself surrounded by bright white light. Know that nothing negative can occur; you will bring in only the highest and the best energy. Picture the person requiring healing as completely perfect and whole. See only perfection and wellness for this person.

2. Begin with your favorite prayer, which is best said aloud. Next, also aloud, state your healing request.

3. State clearly, "thy will be done." Ask only that God's will, and in keeping with His highest purpose, be done.

4. Visualize yourself being used as "God's battery," so that healing energy may be projected through you and into the person. Place a band of white light between you and this person. Visualize it very strongly, since this is extra protection for you. It will keep any negative energy, or "miasma," from entering your body.

5. Still your thoughts. Don't do anything. Just listen to that still, small voice within. Let your higher guidance tell you what needs to be done. Perhaps you will hear nothing at first. But then, usually after a few moments, you will start to receive impressions. Perhaps you will instinctively feel that you should put one hand on the patient's head and another on her back. Perhaps you will be instructed by your higher God consciousness to hold on to the patient's wrist, or to just lightly comb her aura, or electric field, with your hands. You might even feel that you should not touch her at all. Try to mentally "strip away" anything that does not belong in or on the person. For example, imagine a long black sleeve over a leg or arm that needs healing. Mentally strip it away and replace it with white light.

6. At a certain point, you will know that you are finished. Maybe you will know that more sessions are required, or maybe you will realize that this one session was enough. Listen to your feelings, no matter how subtle and wispy the impressions may be. Accept what you receive, and follow the thought.

7. Express gratitude to the healing angels for whatever healing may have occurred—even if you feel that nothing did. Always finish by saying "thank you" to the Creator and His angels.

8. Know in your heart that you are only a conductor. All healing comes from God . . . the God within us all.

When I first became interested in healing, I attempted to find teachers who were excellent healers. I wanted to learn from the best. Unfortunately, I couldn't find anyone who fit the bill. I was, therefore, on my own. I had immediate healing hits and misses.

This, for example, was my first healing "hit": My mom asked me to join her on a visit to her sister Ollie. Aunt Ollie's doctor had informed our family that the dear soul had slipped into a deep coma. If we wished, we could visit her in the hospital to say our last goodbyes.

When my mother and I arrived at Aunt Ollie's bedside, we found her in an unresponsive coma. Because we were alone, I wasn't embarrassed about flexing my new healing muscles. I closed my eyes and asked my inner guidance and highest angels to help with this healing, if it was God's will.

My angels inspired me to understand that I should breathe deeply and hold on to Aunt Ollie's left wrist with my right hand. After about ten minutes, I felt that it was time to release her wrist, thank my angels, and leave. My mom and I both told Aunt Ollie that we loved her and left. When we arrived home about an hour later, the phone was ringing. The doctor was calling to tell us that Aunt Ollie was sitting up in bed and requesting something to eat! He also asked, "What exactly did you both do?"

For months, I doubted that I was at all instrumental in Aunt Ollie's phenomenal healing. Those doubts ended, however, when in a dream I saw myself handing my aunt a new baby. The baby had a big number five on its blanket. I had the impression that my healing request had been granted. I understood that my aunt would be allowed by special heavenly dispensation to live exactly five years from the day of her healing.

Believe it or not, that is exactly what happened. She lived for exactly five years, to the day, after our healing request.

An early healing "miss" occurred when I foolishly misused healing energy.

A very close friend of mine who has diabetes had lost a number of babies shortly after their birth. On this occasion, she had just delivered a baby boy—who was also close to death. Crying on the phone, she said to me, "Joyce, this baby isn't going to make it . . . and my doctor says I can't have any more. I just can't lose this baby. Please pray for us—please!" After feebly trying to say comforting words to her, I hung up the phone. I went into a deep state of prayer and meditation. I spent many hours that night asking God and His healing angels to make the baby well and let him live.

Finally, around three o'clock in the morning, when I felt that my prayers were not being answered, I did something stupid. It was based on ego and lack of faith in God. I've never done it before and will never do it again. I said out loud, "Please take the illness from Joan's baby. Let me have the illness . . . give it to me . . . let the baby live."

A few moments later, I felt a tremendous change in energy. I felt dizzy, nauseated, and weak; I wanted to lie down. When I awoke from a deep sleep a few hours later, I was running a high fever. Every bone, muscle, and cell in my body ached. Every organ was individually in pain. I felt as if I was dying. My husband, Jack, became alarmed and wanted to take me to a hospital emergency room.

I begged him not to because I knew that if he did, I would die there. Instead, I asked him to take me to our friend Dr. Gordon Davidson, a well-known psychic healer and chiropractor.

When Dr. Davidson saw me, he was quiet for a few moments while he attempted to tune in to the situation. Then he spoke. "What did you do, Joyce? Some healing without adequate angelic protection? Don't worry. Healing angels are all around you. They will help to heal you. You're not going to die."

He began trying to help me by using a healing prayer and invoking white light. Then he worked for a long time on my spine, head, and neck. He told me he was clearing and cleaning my aura. I felt sorry that he had to spend so much time and energy to help me, but we both knew it was necessary. After a couple of hours, I started to feel much better and was able to tell him what I had done. With a beatific smile, he said, "You know now that you've broken a cardinal rule of healing. Needless to say, your faith in God and His healing angels should be complete. You should never try to take another's illness on yourself. That's usually a one-way ticket to healer's heaven." I'm happy to say that I came away unscathed, and much wiser. The baby was completely healed and well by the third day of his life. He is now a handsome young chiropractor.

I've also had the experience inadvertently healing someone, while at the same time the person's illness was inadvertently transferred to me. It occurred toward the end of a very crowded but successful live broadcast at my radio station. Many of my longtime listeners were hugging me as they filed out and left. One sweet, rather elderly woman looked at me and said, "Joyce, I'm very sick."

I hugged her and said, "I'm sure God and His healing angels will help you." While I spoke, I felt a tremendous downsurge of energy, as if my life force was being pulled out of my body. I didn't think much of it, and continued to greet my listeners. About three hours later, though, I started to feel great pain in my feet, and my heels started to throb when I attempted to walk. Gradually, the searing pain spread up my legs and through my body, until I realized that I was incapacitated.

I tried to muster up enough energy to heal myself. I went into meditation and was told by one of my angels to relax in a tub of warm water with three handfuls of sea salt. When I did this, I felt nothing at first; my head and body were still overwhelmed with intense pain. Then, slowly, I started to feel a downspiraling of energy. It came into the top of my head, spread throughout my body, and moved out through my feet into the water.

As this occurred, I very clearly heard an angel tell me, "Joyce, you must always be sure to keep up your white shield of angelic protection. This is particularly true when you are meeting and greeting people. It is so easy to transfer an illness when one person is eager to release it and the other is a healer. The protection is always there for you, and will be strengthened if requested.

"When the meeting, greeting, healing, and so forth is over, you must shut down your chakras so your psychic work will temporarily be over. Otherwise, the drain of your energy would continue until either illness or possibly your physical death occurred. This shutting down can be accomplished with the mental request to your higher angelic self, along with your expression of gratitude."

In the years following these experiences, I have been privileged enough to have been a part of many incredible healings. My healing prayers are almost always answered—although not necessarily in the way that I would like them to be.

On my radio and television shows, my audience knows I always have a healing request list. People call or write to me with their requests; I place them on an altar, where a group of us faithfully prays over them. We frequently see or feel the presence of angels during our healing sessions.

When we ask for feedback from our audience, the results are always amazing. Some people have been healed from the most difficult, even "incurable," illnesses. Others have no apparent benefits. I believe that many healings take place only on an inner, deeper level and so are difficult to discern. Sometimes people have been completely healed, but then have passed away shortly after. I don't think we should ever second-guess God. We should always say, "Thy will be done."

I have also had the privilege of receiving amazing healings myself. Two occurred at St. Anne's Shrine at Isle La Motte, near Burlington, Vermont. A few years ago, I was losing the use of my right hand and experiencing intense pain in my thumb and palm. X rays showed an accumulation of extra bone at the base of my thumb. When medical treatment and acupuncture did not help me, I decided to go to the Vermont shrine.

There I walked up to the thirty-foot-high statue of the Blessed Mother, which faces majestically out to Lake Champlain. After standing for a few minutes, I heard an angel say to me, "Walk around the statue three times, with faith in your heart, and your hand will be healed."

I did as I was told. I'm thrilled to say that within one month, my hand was absolutely perfect. X rays no longer showed any accumulation of extra bone!

The next summer, I developed the same problem in my left hand. I returned to the shrine, and that hand was also completely healed.

photo credit: Jack Keller

To Ease Stress and Worry

Angel of Tranquillity
Fill me with peace
Unfurrow my brow
Let my worrying cease!

Recommendations to eliminate stress and stop worrying:

PRAYER   In your prayers, ask your highest angels for what the Bible calls "the peace that passes all understanding."

MANTRA   Use this mantra whenever you start experiencing any stress or tension.

MEDITATION   Begin meditation with deep, rhythmic breathing. See yourself floating on a comfortable, supportive cloud, surrounded by nurturing, attentive angels.

ATTITUDE   Your attitude should reflect the old adage, "Today is the tomorrow we worried about yesterday." Think of a beautiful white duck. This creature knows how to let things simply "roll off."

ATMOSPHERE   To destress your atmosphere, use the aromatherapy fragrance jasmine. Place a few drops of the oil on a light bulb before using it. Better still, purchase a clay or ceramic lightbulb fragrance ring; put this around the upper portion of the bulb and put several drops of the oil into the groove or depression.

SUBSTANCES   Take elm or mimulus Bach Flower Remedy; in a very stressful situation, take Rescue Remedy. Drink valerian, chamomile, sassafras, or kava-kava tea. Use eucalyptus or pineapple twist aromatherapy oil.

CRYSTALS & GEMS   Hold a rhodochrosite crystal in your hand to release stress. (Carry one in your pocket for easy access during stressful times.)

To Stay Young

Angel of Youth
Angel sublime
Touch my entire being
Keep my cells in their prime!

Recommendations for staying young:

PRAYER   In prayers, ask your angels to help you slow down or even reverse the aging process.

MANTRA   Use this mantra when you begin the day, as you prepare for the day, or whenever you wish to look your best.

MEDITATION   In meditation, see yourself as you looked at your very best, whatever age that may have been. Concentrate first on a great photo of yourself. In addition, keep that photo in a place where you can see it as you get ready for each day.

ATTITUDE   Your attitude should reflect only "young" ideas. Never use the word *old* in regard to anything about yourself. Your cells will respond to whatever you say and believe.

ATMOSPHERE   Use Feng Shui to place everything in your home or business in the proper location for maximum energy. Place your bed so that you can see the door. Prepare and eat meals where you can see out a window, for as much light or angelic energy as possible.

SUBSTANCES   Make an herbal pouch of the herb suma and the Chinese herb shizandra to place under your pillow. Consider taking DHEA, ginseng (for men), fo-ti, and bee pollen. Women who are menopausal can be helped by eating soybeans and by using natural wild yam cream, which contains diosgenin.

CRYSTALS & GEMS   Carry a piece of chrysocolla with you, and use it for meditation.

For Weight Loss

Angel of Physicality
Angel divine
Increase my self-control
Let body perfection be mine!

Recommendations for successful, permanent weight loss:

PRAYER   Use as a prayer, "Less of me, Lord, and more of thee."

MANTRA   Use this mantra before meals and whenever you are hungry or wish to snack.

MEDITATION   Visualize yourself at your ideal weight. Say aloud what you would like that weight to be.

ATTITUDE   Know that your prayers and mantras are heard, and that the angels will help reinforce your will power. Be aware of overall improvements in your metabolism and well-being.

ATMOSPHERE   Place a mirror wherever you find yourself eating. This may be difficult if there are others around, of course, but if you watch yourself eating, you will definitely eat less!

SUBSTANCES   Bladderwrack, thallus, chitosan (to absorb fat,) fennel seed, chickweed, and sea wrack are herbs that are most helpful as dietary supplements. In addition, use kelp, lecithin, apple cider vinegar, and B_6. Aromatherapy oils that help are tropical mango and honeysuckle mango. Many people are also helped by the Chinese herbs poria, semenlitchi, fructusmeliae, and toosendan.

CRYSTALS & GEMS   Carry lapis lazuli and celestite for your metabolism. Also, wear a piece of chrysocolla as close as possible to the thyroid area of your neck.

To Help Abused People

Angels of Mercy
Angels with hearts
Stop all abuse
Before it starts.

Recommendations to stop all forms of abuse:

PRAYER   If you are being abused, or know of someone who is being abused, contact the police. If the situation continues, your prayers should include requests for the most powerful angels to intervene and protect. Ask for the angels to come in and "take action" against the abuser, so that all abuse will abruptly stop. Note: This also works magic against muggers and other criminals.

MANTRA   Repeat this powerful mantra, which has been known to stop abuse before it even begins.

MEDITATION   In meditation, visualize a wall of protection that will separate the abused person from the abuser.

ATTITUDE   Know that there is never an excuse or reasonable reason for abuse. Leave if you feel that abuse is imminent. Always seek human help as well.

ATMOSPHERE   To create the best atmosphere for angelic assistance, if it seems that abuse is unavoidable and imminent, clearly and strongly visualize a wall between the abused and the abuser. Also, use the mantra.

SUBSTANCES   The most helpful Bach Flower Remedies are centaury, crab apple, gorse, rock water, walnut, and Rescue Remedy. The most helpful aromatherapy fragrance is mandarin.

CRYSTALS & GEMS   Crystals that can be placed on your altar or held are citrine (to bolster self-esteem) or sugilite, worn close to the body.

After Surgery or an Accident

Angels of Healing
Take cosmic thread
Sew up the damage
From toe to head!

Recommendations to speed healing after a trauma:

PRAYER   In your prayers, express gratitude for the expedited healing.

MANTRA   Use this mantra whenever the need for healing arises.

MEDITATION   Clearly see the angelic surgeons working miracles on this person.

ATTITUDE   If you are requesting assistance for someone else, you can use yourself as a battery. Before beginning, ask for protection for yourself. Place your hands a few inches away from the person, or actually place your hands on his head. Allow the healing energy to flow through you to him. When you feel the session is over, rinse your hands and wrists with cold water, and express gratitude for angelic assistance.

ATMOSPHERE   Use aromatherapy fragrances of pine, peppermint, and freesia rain.

SUBSTANCES   Use the Bach Flower Rescue Remedy.

CRYSTALS & GEMS   The most healing crystals are jade and hematite.

Through the grace of God and His healing angels, I've had the most remarkable experiences with adults, children, animals, and self-healing. As Jesus said, "All these things I do, you shall do also."

I've been honored enough to have been in the presence of some world-famous healers, including Katherine Kuhlman, who passed away in 1976. When I witnessed her healing services at a church in Pittsburgh, I realized that miraculous healings were being granted. Over a number of services, I saw a child's leg grow long and straight enough for her to abandon her brace. I saw a blind man's vision given back to him. I saw crooked spines become straight. I have witnessed many healings in services conducted by other healers as well.

I find that animals and children respond amazingly well to healing. Perhaps it is because they are so open and trusting. For example, one day my angels made it clear to me that I should go outside and stand at my curb—as if I was waiting for something or someone. I felt foolish, but I listened to my angelic guidance.

So there I was, standing close to the street, waiting and watching. Suddenly, from my left, I saw a red Cadillac approaching. Simultaneously, the adorable little white poodle that lived across the street came bounding across his lawn and into the street. I raised my hand to stop the car while also shouting at Nipper to stop. But it was no use. The dog was hit and lay dying in the street. Neighbors came out. We all saw Nipper take his last breath, blood pouring out of his body. His owner, Mrs. Nebrock, covered him and tearfully said, "Poor Nipper. We all loved you."

Then, without realizing it, I said, "Wait. Don't cover him." I intuitively began listening to the directions of my healing angel. I knelt down, placed my hands over the dog, and silently prayed. I asked for the Holy Spirit to enter him, heal him, and make him whole again. I tried to see him completely well and perfectly healthy. I tried to use my hands as batteries to help recharge him with angelic life force.

Suddenly, to the shock and surprise of all of us, he raised his head and looked around. After a few minutes, he sat. Shortly thereafter, he jumped up and ran home!

I'm sure you can be a channel of healing also. The most important first step is your wish to help others. Recognize the power of prayer in your everyday life, and in your healing efforts. Have faith in your heart. Know that all healing prayers are heard. They are just not always answered as quickly as we would like, or necessarily in the way we had in mind. *Prayer and faith are at the root of all God-centered angelic healing.*

To Overcome Depression

Angels of Joy
Angels of gladness
Lift the clouds
Get rid of all sadness!

Recommendations to help overcome depression:

PRAYER   Always consult a medical expert. In your prayers, turn to your angels with trust. Know that help is at hand.

MANTRA   Use this mantra throughout the day.

MEDITATION   Visualize yourself lying on the sand on a warm, cloudy day. As you relax completely, see the clouds dissipate. Look up and see only a clear blue, bright sky. You feel tremendous uplift and joy. You realize that you are replacing sad feelings with joy and joie de vivre. Do this for five minutes, three times a day.

ATTITUDE   Your attitude should reflect others' negativity away from yourself. Reject your own negative thoughts, too, as you realize you no longer wish to be depressed.

ATMOSPHERE   Lift your atmosphere with the use of the aromatherapy oils bergamot and melissa. These can be used with a dispenser.

SUBSTANCES   Bach Flower Remedies agrimony, gentian, gorse, mustard, and oak will quickly lift you out of depression. Also, according to the August

3, 1996, *British Medical Journal,* the herb hypericum, which is also known as St. John's wort, has successfully helped many people with depression. Again, always consult a medical expert.

CRYSTALS & GEMS   Carry an aquamarine stone with you at all times. Know that things can always be worse, and will soon be improving for the better!

For Restful Sleep or to Cure Insomnia

Angels of Repose
Angels of Sleep
Help me to rest fully
Long, restful, and deep.

Recommendations for restful sleep, or to help cure insomnia:

PRAYER   Before going to sleep, pray for protection while "out of body." Know that angels will protect and keep you.

MANTRA   Keep repeating the mantra until you fall asleep.

MEDITATION   As you meditate before you sleep, see in your mind's eye angels preparing a place for you. When your very comfortable bed is ready, envision one angel smiling and motioning you into this special bed. Allow your angels to cover you with whatever you will find most comfortable for your repose. Feel one angel gently close your eyelids.

ATTITUDE   Your attitude should be one of knowing that you cannot stay awake. Make a practice of falling asleep at will, and sleeping for as long as you wish. Your angels will help you accomplish this if you request it with sincerity.

ATMOSPHERE   The aromatherapy fragrances that will help the work of the angels are neroli and sweet dreams.

SUBSTANCES   The herbs that will help you are passionflower, kava-kava, and the Chinese herb an mien pien. The supplement melatonin may also work well.

CRYSTALS & GEMS   The crystals malachite and lepidolite, kept under your pillow, will also work wonders.

To Lift Despair and Sadness

Angels of Compassion
I'm tired of trying
Help me feel joy
No more tears or crying.

Recommendations to overcome despair and sadness:

PRAYER Ask in your prayers that extra doors of angelic assistance be opened for you.

MANTRA Repeat this mantra slowly whenever sad feelings sweep over you.

MEDITATION Imagine a door swinging open and a team of beautiful, loving angels approaching you. As they surround you, realize that they are smiling and reaching their hands out to you. As they touch you, feel immediately uplifted, and peace sweeping over you.

ATTITUDE Strive to forget the cause of your sadness and replace it with uplift from your angels.

ATMOSPHERE Your atmosphere will be uplifted further by burning cherry or strawberry incense.

SUBSTANCES The Bach Flower Remedies agrimony, gentian, gorse, mustard, and Rescue Remedy will help the angels lift and clear your aura.

CRYSTALS & GEMS Carry a pink quartz crystal close to your heart.

For Astral Travel

Angels of Confinement
I can't get past the door
Please touch my soul
Help my spirit to soar!

Recommendations to assist astral travel:

PRAYER   In your prayers, ask for freedom and liberation from the confinement of your physical body. (In both astral projection and death there is separation and projection of the nonphysical from the physical body. The difference is that when we physically die, we cannot return to our physical body.)

MANTRA   Repeat this mantra three times to help project your spirit astrally. Let your spirit soar!

MEDITATION   See yourself allowing angels to help you project yourself up and out of your physical body. Ask these angels to protect your body as you astrally project from it. Allow yourself to soar freely, easily, and joyfully with them. Know that you are connected to your body with your invisible "silver thread," that you can go as far as you would like to, and that no harm can come to you. Steady practice of this technique will bring greater and greater control.

ATTITUDE   Know that you can experience a miracle!

ATMOSPHERE   Your out-of-body travel will be enhanced by burning frankincense.

SUBSTANCES   The Bach Flower Remedy heather will help you in your soaring.

CRYSTALS & GEMS   A rose quartz crystal will help bring you comfort. A moldavite crystal will help you leave your body more easily, and return smoothly.

To Overcome Anger

Angels of Peace
Please stop feelings hot
Keep us from saying
And doing things we should not!

Recommendations to overcome anger:

PRAYER   Ask in prayer for immediate angelic help in overcoming your anger.

MANTRA   Repeat this mantra while pressing your fingertips into your solar plexus, which is often a seat of unexpressed anger.

MEDITATION   When you feel yourself losing control and becoming angry, count to ten. Breathe in slowly, filling your lungs completely; exhale slowly and deeply through your nose. Continue this deep breathing.

ATTITUDE   Allow the angels to work with you, calm you down, and bring you serenity. That's their specialty!

ATMOSPHERE   If you have a tendency to be agitated or angry, try to eliminate the color red from your surroundings. Bring in peaceful greens and blues. Use the aromatherapy fragrance frangipani, or burn strawberry incense.

SUBSTANCES   To stay in control, use agrimony, impatiens, or willow Bach Flower Remedies.

CRYSTALS & GEMS   Carry an aquamarine gemstone with you. Rub it when you need to gain control.

To Overcome Loneliness

Angels of Companionship
Come fill my room
Replace this empty feeling
With love, to replace gloom!

Recommendations to help overcome loneliness:

PRAYER   Your prayers should be said while burning a pink candle.

MANTRA   Repeat this mantra after drinking a large glass of water.

MEDITATION   Center your meditation in your heart chakra. Visualize pink rays of light coming out from your heart, and radiating out for a distance of at least two feet from your body. Practice this technique until you gain enough control to do it at will. Use it whenever you are feeling lonely. You may also use it when you are with people whom you wish to attract to you.

ATTITUDE   Your attitude, when you wish others to find you attractive, should be loving and warm. Mentally work at bringing down barriers and blocks that may have worked against you in the past.

ATMOSPHERE   Use the aromatherapy oils jasmine and bergamot.

SUBSTANCES   For antiloneliness, uplifting substances are the heather, mustard, and water violet Bach Flower Remedies.

CRYSTALS & GEMS   Keep a pink quartz crystal with you at all times. It will help absorb those feelings, and project love.

To Heal Emotional Trauma

Angels who Repair Trauma
From realms heavenly blue
Please mend my soul
With your angelic glue.

Recommendations to help heal emotional trauma—the death of a loved one, divorce, or any loss that plummets you into despair:

PRAYER In times of serious trauma, when you may feel that your heart and soul are being torn in different directions, you must make as strong an effort as possible to get yourself centered. Nothing helps more than prayer. Even though angels always help in times of distress, it's important to express your need for assistance. Let your prayers reflect this.

MANTRA Use this mantra to let the angels know your needs. Say it aloud as often as necessary for soothing peace and angelic healing.

MEDITATION In meditation, visualize a large, loving, motherly angel holding you on her lap. As you are cradled, she whispers healing, nurturing words into your ears. You can't quite hear the words, but they go deep into your soul to heal your trauma.

ATTITUDE Your attitude should be one of optimism. Once the healing process begins, try to start over.

ATMOSPHERE Create an atmosphere of regeneration and wellness. If, for example, photos cause you pain, put them away for a while. Don't listen to sad music that may cause you to live through unpleasant memories. Use berga-mont or neroli aromatherapy oil to help the angels work with you.

SUBSTANCES   The Bach Flower Remedies that will help heal your emo-tions are Star of Bethlehem, rock rose, larch, gorse, gentian, and agrimony. Remember, Rescue Remedy is always the best Bach Flower Remedy for trauma.

CRYSTALS & GEMS   Meditate with a pink quartz crystal.

For Eye Health and Healing

Angels of Vision
Who help us see clearly
Heal, protect my eyes
That I need so dearly!

Recommendations for healing or improving the health of eyes:

PRAYER   Always check with your eye doctor. In your prayers, ask the angels of vision to improve the health of your eyes.

MANTRA   Use this mantra in conjunction with your prayers and meditation.

MEDITATION   In meditation, imagine your eyes as having perfect vision. For example, if you have cataracts, see the angels of vision working on your eyes. Visualize them helping to correct the problem. Try to see the instruments that they are using.

ATTITUDE   Know that miracles are possible. Expect your vision to be improved. A positive attitude will always assist our angelic helpers.

ATMOSPHERE   Be protective of your eyes. If you are out in bright sunshine or snow, wear UV-blocking sunglasses. Use sunglasses when you drive. Do not work continuously under fluorescent lights, since they gradually destroy vitamin A and are tiring to your eyes. If you work at a computer, give your eyes frequent rests. Do eye exercises once a day, rotating your eyes clockwise, then counterclockwise. Practice "palming" whenever your eyes feel tired or irritated: Rapidly rub your hands together until they feel quite warm, then quickly cup them over your closed eyes for a few moments. It's also important to visit your ophthalmologist regularly.

SUBSTANCES   Beta-carotene, a non-toxic form of vitamin A, will help strengthen your eyes, as will supplements of bilberry and euphrasia. I strongly recommend looking for a supplement that contains lutein for an extra boost to eye health. Eye irritations can often be relieved with an eye bath of eyebright, which is another name for euphrasia. Cool euphrasia or chamomile tea bags placed on tired or irritated eyes usually bring quick relief. Again always check with your eye doctor.

CRYSTALS & GEMS   The best crystal for eye support and healing is a clear quartz crystal.

To Eliminate Alcohol or Drug Abuse

Angels of Power
No alcohol or drug use
Free me from temptation
And all forms of abuse.

Recommendations for the elimination of alcohol or drug abuse:

PRAYER   Ask in sincere prayer for greater willpower. God and His angels will help you if you truly wish to stop substance abuse. It is not easy, but with the help of these powerful angels, it is possible.

MANTRA   When faced with temptation, use this powerful angel mantra.

MEDITATION   In meditation, see yourself standing straight and tall, with your greatest addiction crushed under your feet.

ATTITUDE   Your attitude should be one of wanting success over temptation more than anything else in the universe. You will feel the support of the angels; give them a chance to help you. Let them work with you.

ATMOSPHERE   Create an atmosphere absolutely free of temptation. Your atmosphere should also include a support system such as Alcoholics Anonymous.

SUBSTANCES   Use gorse, aspen, and cerato Bach Flower Remedies for effective help at the emotional level.

CRYSTALS & GEMS   Carry a kunzite crystal, also known as pink spodumene, for support.

Business and Finance

For Success in Business

Business Angel
Wearing wings and tweed
Help bring this situation
The success I need!

Recommendations for success in business:

PRAYER   In your prayers, ask for the success you desire. You have a right to ask to be blessed with abundance from the universe. Ask that it be for the greater good of all concerned.

MANTRA   Use this mantra three times a day.

MEDITATION   In meditation, see clearly the specific type of success you desire. Add as much detail to your visualization as possible.

ATTITUDE   Know in your heart, with simple faith, that you deserve this success, and that you appreciate the angel's assistance.

ATMOSPHERE   Use Feng Shui to encourage success. Create symbols of money above the area where you work. Burn a green seven-day candle (in a bowl of water, for safety reasons).

SUBSTANCES   Use cerato, elm, and larch Bach Flower Remedies. Wear angelica or bay fragrances.

CRYSTALS & GEMS   Use citrine or clear quartz for power and success.

For Prosperity

Angel of Abundance
Bringing milk and honey
My coffer needs
To be filled with money!

Recommendations for increased prosperity:

PRAYER   Ask with an attitude of simple faith for the floodgates of universal abundance to be opened to you, and for all that you need to come pouring into your life. Express gratitude for all that will be forthcoming.

MANTRA   Use this mantra at least five times a day.

MEDITATION   Clearly see money flowing into your home and office. See tons of hundred-dollar bills flowing in through every window and door.

ATTITUDE   Write out your request for increased prosperity, as specifically as possible. Fold it in half and place it on your altar, under a glass of water. If you need a hundred thousand dollars a year, state this. Don't be shy! Go for it. You may be pleasantly surprised. Be optimistic, and don't set ceilings or limitations on what the universe may be able to bring you.

ATMOSPHERE   Burn a seven-day green candle (in a bowl of water, for safety reasons). Pray near it, to attract the highest angelic energy.

SUBSTANCES   Use the larch Bach Flower Remedy and angelica or peppermint fragrance.

CRYSTALS & GEMS   Meditate with citrine quartz crystals.

To Find Employment

Angels of Work
Send some great employment
I need income
For life's enjoyment!

Recommendations to help find employment:

PRAYER Know that your prayers will be heard, and that astral wheels will turn to help you.

MANTRA Repeat this mantra when searching for leads as well as before interviews.

MEDITATION See in your mind's eye a check written out to you. See clearly what the amount is, and know that it will soon be coming in on a regular basis. It will also help to actually write a check to yourself for the amount that you would like to be paid weekly.

ATTITUDE Maintain an attitude of joyful expectation—with the awareness, however, that you will also take whatever steps are necessary to bring about employment. This includes the possibility of retraining or further education. Send out those resumés and check the newspapers or employment office. Remember, finding a job is a full-time occupation.

ATMOSPHERE Burn a seven-day green candle (in a bowl of water, for safety reasons). Place the check that you have written to yourself under that bowl of water. If you need further positive reinforcement, read books such as Catherine Ponder's *Keys to Prosperity*.

SUBSTANCES   Use the larch, clematis, and wild oat Bach Flower Remedies to increase angelic energy.

CRYSTALS & GEMS   Carry citrine quartz or peridot, which has the reputation of being able to open doors to prosperity.

Death and Mourning

Preparation for Death

Angels of Transition
Angels of Death
Prepare the path
As [name] takes his/her last breath.

Recommendations to help prepare a person for the death experience:

PRAYER At the time of a person's or animal's death, ask in prayer that his path be surrounded with God's white light.

MANTRA Repeat this angel mantra. The word *om* or other sacred names are also very helpful.

MEDITATION Visualize four angels, one in each corner of the bed or room.

ATTITUDE Maintain an attitude of support and encouragement, rather than despair and grief. It always helps to say, "Thy will be done."

ATMOSPHERE Sprinkle either holy water or Florida water around the bed and room to contribute to a helpful atmosphere.

SUBSTANCES For all creatures in this situation, or those who are about to lose a loved one, use the Bach Flower Rescue Remedy and aspen.

CRYSTALS & GEMS Hold an amethyst or azurite gem because they are able to take in negative energy and give back positive.

Angels at My Father's Deathbed

After I stood by my dad's bedside for quite a few days and nights, the energy in the room changed radically; it seemed to become charged with electricity. I felt as if every hair on my head and body was standing straight up. I realized that he was about to pass away.

Then I looked up and away from my dad and saw four angelic beings—one standing at each corner of his bed. Emanating from these beings was a warm, loving, all-encompassing comfort. As each extended an arm toward my dad, he breathed one last deep, throaty breath. I saw what looked like a puffy white cloud rise from the upper part of his body. It ascended toward the ceiling, then dissipated slowly. When I looked back at his bed, I realized that the four angels had left with him.

I unmistakably felt an unseen arm around me, giving me a small hug. Most of my sadness was replaced with the comfort of knowing that my dear dad was in very good hands.

For Deceased Loved Ones

Angels of Heaven
Angels of the Sun
Watch over [name]
Cradle my loved one.

Recommendations for receiving protection and guidance for a deceased loved one:

PRAYER   As you pray, burn a white candle for your loved one. Ask that she be surrounded with the highest, brightest white light in God's universe. Send "lovegrams," or heartfelt messages of love and support. If possible, have a photo of your loved one nearby.

MANTRA   Use this mantra whenever you feel sad, or feel the need to make contact with your loved one.

MEDITATION   In meditation, try to see your departed loved one surrounded by the brightest, strongest white light you can visualize. This always helps to light the path.

ATTITUDE   Maintain an attitude of support and love; grief might keep your loved one from escalating in the postdeath experience. Such an attitude is not always easy, but it is important: Your sadness will almost always be shared by your departed loved ones, which is not in their best interest.

ATMOSPHERE   Burn white candles, which are perceived in the spirit world as messages of love and support for your deceased loved ones. In addition, burn patchouli incense alongside their photos to send love and support.

SUBSTANCES   Aromatherapy fragrances that help people on both sides of the veil include angelica and sweet dreams.

CRYSTALS & GEMS   Carry a clear crystal if you wish to send messages of love to those who are deceased. A quartz crystal can project as well as absorb energy.

For Help in Times of Mourning

Angels of Separation
Who help handle grief
Let my emotions
Feel healing and relief.

Recommendations for receiving help in times of mourning or grief:

PRAYER   Pray for uplift and understanding. Ask your angels to show you the "big" picture—which can alleviate a great deal of mourning and grief.

MANTRA   Use this mantra to instantly help change and uplift your energies.

MEDITATION   Visualize yourself bathed in warm, beautiful, emerald green healing light. Feel the most loving, tender angels sitting with you and wrapping their arms gently around you. Feel the uplift and peace that comes from their presence.

ATTITUDE   Your attitude should be that of a small child who needs the tender loving care of a parent: Allow yourself to be healed as angels come to you; do not put up barriers or resistance to their assistance.

ATMOSPHERE   Enhance your atmosphere by diffusing bergamot, Oriental dew, violet, honeysuckle meadows, and wild strawberry aromatherapy oils.

SUBSTANCES   Use the Bach Flower Remedies gentian, gorse, mustard, Star of Bethlehem, and Rescue Remedy.

CRYSTALS & GEMS   Lift your vibrations by meditating and carrying a pink quartz crystal.

After a Loss

Angels of Mercy
With the power you wield
Touch my being
Let my soul be healed.

Recommendations for healing the psyche after suffering the loss of a person or animal who has been loved deeply:

PRAYER   Simply ask in prayer for relief from your pain.

MANTRA   Use the angel mantra. Angels know your needs, and even if you don't see them, perhaps you can feel their loving presence.

MEDITATION   Envision, as clearly as possible, the angels of mercy surrounding you and giving you support and healing. They are there because you have called upon them.

ATTITUDE   Open your heart and mind to allow the healing of the angels to begin. The more often you repeat this process, the more complete the healing will be.

ATMOSPHERE   Use neroli and bergamot aromatherapy oils. Use the Bach Flower Remedies agrimony, gentian, mustard, and Star of Bethlehem. For immediate distress or emergencies, use Bach Flower Rescue Remedy.

SUBSTANCES   Pine is the substance that will quickly and easily bring the healing assistance of angels. The best method is to walk near pine trees, allowing their fragrance to permeate your being; if this is impossible, inhale tincture of pine oil or take a pine oil bath. A pine sachet or envelope under your pillow will work wonders, too. It's also very helpful to take a clean white handkerchief and leave it outside overnight. The material will be permeated by a mystical morning dew. Hold this hankie close to your heart when you desire angelic presence. You may also place it on top of your pillow while you are sleeping. Expect angelic miracles!

CRYSTALS & GEMS   Hold a clear quartz crystal or amethyst in your hand. Keep one in your pocket for those times when you feel you need angelic support.

To Find Missing People, Animals or Items

Angels of Recovery
Who seek, find and return
The location of _____
Is what I need to discern.

Recommendations for finding missing people, animals or items:

PRAYER   Picture in your mind's eye, as clearly as possible, the missing person(s), animal(s) or items. Ask with simple faith for you to be shown while awake or in a dream, where they are located.

MANTRA   Recite this mantra throughout the day, and before going to sleep.

MEDITATION   Each time you use this mantra, visualize or try to see as clearly as possible who or what you are trying to find.

ATTITUDE   Have an attitude of confidence and loving receptivity. You know in your heart, mind, and spirit that your location attempts will be successful.

ATMOSPHERE   Create an atmosphere of loving receptivity in your home or office. Try to have a clear photo of the person(s), animal(s) or items that are missing. Look into the eyes of the photo, try to perceive an impression about where they are located. Your angels will help you.

SUBSTANCES   Burn patchouli incense, and use red rose aromatherapy oil.

CRYSTALS & GEMS   A small piece or black obsidian held in your hand can be used to focus your attention, so that you may recieve a clear answer as you gaze into the stone.

The following is an example of how angels can help us find a missing person: A woman called into my radio show, and said, "My father has Alzheimer's disease, and he's missing." I quickly sent out of silent prayer, asking to be shown his location.

Within a couple of seconds, I was intuitively told that he was in "Florida." What was strange, though, was that I didn't have the impression that it was a tropical location. Also, I felt that it was someplace having to do with transportation, and that he was sitting, and waiting to be picked up.

My listener called me on the next show, and said the following. "Joyce, I told my husband what you said. He reminded me that my father had old cronies living in a small town in upstate New York. It is a town known as Florida, New York! We got into our car, drove upstate. We found my Dad sitting on a bench in the bus terminal in that town. No wonder I didn't see palm trees when the angels showed me his location!

To Assist Those Confined

Angels of Confinement
I can't get past the door
Please touch my soul
Help my spirit to soar!

Recommendations to assist those confined to hospitals, etc.

STEP 1   In your prayers, ask for freedom and liberation from the confinement of your physical body.

STEP 2   Repeating this mantra three times will help your spirit to soar!

STEP 3   See yourself allowing angels to come to you, to help project yourself up and out of your physical body. Ask these angels to project your body, as you astrally project out and away from it. Allow yourself to soar freely, easily, and joyfully with them. Know that you are connected to your body with your invisible "silver cord," and that you can go as far as you would like to, and that no harm can come to you. Steady practice of this technique will bring greater and greater control.

STEP 4   Your attitude is that you know you can experience a miracle!

STEP 5   This out-of-body travel will be enhanced by your burning frankincense incense.

STEP 6   The Bach Flower Remedy, heather, will help you in your soaring.

STEP 7   A rose quartz crystal will help to bring you comfort. A molavite crystal will help you leave your body more easily, and return smoothly.

INDEX